LOVE WITHOUT LIMITS

LOVE

WITHOUT LIMITS

Jesus' Radical Vision for Love
with <u>No</u> Exceptions

Jacqueline A. Bussie

LOVE WITHOUT LIMITS
Jesus' Radical Vision for Love with No Exceptions

Cover design: Brad Norr
Design and Typesetting: PerfecType, Nashville, TN

Print ISBN: 978-1-5064-4688-2
eBook ISBN: 978-1-5064-4689-9

The paper used in this publication meets the minimum requirements of American National Standard for Information Sciences — Permanence of Paper for Printed Library Materials, ANSI Z329.48-1984.

Manufactured in the U.S.A.

To Love—may you triumph everywhere and always

ACKNOWLEDGMENTS

This book had a difficult birth, which makes me all the more grateful to every person who helped it reach the light. Here are my many thank-yous.

To my mom—for being my first teacher of a love without limits. I love you and miss you. Always.

To my marvelous husband, Matthew—for loving me the way only a best friend can. There is no me without you.

To the entire awesome Fortress Press team—especially Beth Lewis, Tim Blevins, Will Bergkamp, Tony Jones, and Mari Sharpe—for adopting this book and embracing its message . . . every single word.

To my amazing Facebook squad—for the solidarity and for finding this book a new publisher in only twenty-four hours.

To my agent, Greg Daniel—for standing by me when I made hard decisions that affected us both.

To the Jentel Foundation—for the generous artist's residency in August 2017. It was writer's heaven!

To Concordia College—for the sabbatical; to my Concordia colleagues—for being such a caring and committed community.

To my surrogate parents, Helen Beth Kuhens and Tony Abbott—and their awesome spouses, Galen Kuhens and Susan Abbott—for adopting me and being life-changing mentors.

To Caryn Riswold, Amanda Altobell, Leslie Bellwood, Fauzia Haider, Rick and Bobbi Henderson, Pete and Libby Slade, Kathy and David Hunstad, Caroline Watkins, Deborah Slice, Jill Hunter Dale, Karen Anderson Hlavacek, Mary Anderson, Amy Watkin,

Jane Ahlin, Michael Larson, Bill and Pam Thompson, Marty Stortz, Rahuldeep Gill, Homayra Ziad, and Raymond Rea—for the gift of your friendship and the many ways you helped with this book. You all are beautiful humans.

To Sarah McIlvried, Katie Grooms, Abbie Carver, and Carolyn May—for the solidarity, sisters.

To Sarah, Mac, Perry, and Perry—for the friendship and the use of your beautiful casita. And the grapefruit!

To Tom Schlotterback—for convincing me to follow my call to Concordia.

To Carol Kapaun Ratchenski—for telling me to never back down from the truth and to never "shut up and disappear."

To the entire Myers, Brock, and Kmiec clans—for being such good family to me and to each other.

To my original publisher—for believing from the start that I had this book inside me. You were so right . . . and I forgive the rest.

To my students, past, present, and future—for teaching me and inspiring me.

To Fargo—for accepting this southern girl and teaching me that every winter can be survived.

To Jesus—for teaching me to call BS on any love with asterisks or exceptions, even my own.

To the ELCA, my church home—thank you for being a church that proclaims God's love without limits.

And finally, to everyone in my life who's shown me love—for making me the person I am today. I love because you first loved me.

TABLE OF CONTENTS

INTRODUCTION

This book was censored. To my shock, the Christian publisher that paid me handsomely to write it—and had agreed to its subject of God's radical love—deemed two chapters "theologically out of bounds." I was asked to cut specific true stories—stories expressing my love and appreciation for my Muslim friends and LGBTQ friends—because they were "not in line with the values of the majority of their readers."

I refused.

In turn, the press terminated my contract. They insisted they owned the rights to the book because they had paid me to write it. If I wanted to publish the book elsewhere, I—or another press—would have to pay back every cent.

My heart broke. Not for the book or for me or for the tens of thousands of dollars I'd lost, but for my Muslim and LGBTQ friends whose stories had been censored. Power had asked me to sell them out. To—quite literally—delete them. Of course, if I had done so, every word of this book would have shriveled into a lie.

The situation's irony reared up on its hind legs and stared me down. Think about it: I wrote a book about how people of faith are called to love with no exceptions, asterisks, or limits. And then my publisher asked me to make exceptions, add asterisks, and set limits. It was my publisher who had come up with the original subtitle: *Jesus' Radical Vision for a Love with No Exceptions.* Seriously, I couldn't make this stuff up. If I hadn't been crying so hard, I might've laughed.

But wait, there's more. In the very book my Christian publisher found offensive, I had written: "How will you know when your *agape*-love is as thick and wide and titanic as God wants? Well, if Jesus' own life is any indication, once you completely offend other people. Jesus wants us to distend our love so far, its swollen face will completely scandalize the VIPs, government officials, members of our own family, and especially the most powerful people within our own religious tradition. . . . Basically, if you annoy the heck out of the powerful, then you will know that your love has dilated sufficiently."

My book was barely born, and this world had already proved its message right. Nothing is more scandalous and subversive than a love without limits.

Our society is more polarized and divided than ever. I know you feel it. That breath-catch at the holiday dinner table when Uncle Joe mentions politics; that nausea-surge in your gut when ex-friends decimate each other on Facebook. We don't talk; we shout and insult. We don't listen; we silence and censor. We don't leave our social media silos; we follow only our own team. I am as guilty of this as anyone. I'm sorry. The best I can do is try not to be a part of it any longer, and do what writers do—write. Write about my journey to love bigger and better, and those who taught me how.

This book is my life's love letter—to you and to everyone else. Thank you for reading it—*especially* if you don't agree with all of it. As I tell my students, understanding and agreement are *not* the same thing; they never were. Love demands only the first, not the second. If you don't agree with this book and you keep reading anyway in order to understand, you are courageous. You care. You are everything this torn-in-half world needs right now. I thank you.

If we disagree, we must hate each other, right? No. This is our culture's lie du jour, and we must resist with our very lives. Before you read this book, know this: if you disagree with me on any social or political issue, I love you. If you agree with me, I love you. If you're the publisher who censored this book, I love you. If you're a Republican, I love you. If you're a Democrat or an Independent, I love you. If you are straight or LGBTQ, I love you. If your skin is brown, white, or black, I love you. If you hate this book, I love you anyway; if you love it, I love you, too. If you're Christian, I love you. If you're Muslim, I love you. If you're an atheist, I love you. If you're Sikh, Hindu, Jewish, Baha'i, or Native American, I love you. If you're an American citizen, I love you. If you're Syrian, Iraqi, French, or Kenyan, I love you. If you're a refugee or an immigrant, I love you. I. Love. You. All. Period. No exceptions—as badly as some days I want to make them.

One day while writing this book, I saw an engraved woodcarving above a church door. It said EXCLUDE NO ONE. If God's love had a Twitter handle, this would be it. I vow to do my best to follow the love advice of @ExcludeNoOne. Not because I'm a good person or righteous or faithful. No, simply because I'm bone-tired of living in a mean and hateful world. And let's get real: I'm part of the reason it's like that. I'm really lousy at a love without limits. Too many days to count, I fail with flying colors. But the important thing is, I refuse to give up. I vow to keep trying.

And more than anything, I hope you'll join me.

Some stories in this world never get told or sold. Why? Because people at the top know if they allow us folks down below to tell them, we'd find out our power is greater than we'd ever dared hope or dream. All our love-without-limits stories fall into this category, which is why we must fight like hell to tell them.

So, people in power—and all who try to be big bad wolves—bring it on. Huff and puff away at our love without limits. In the end, what is true will turn your face blue.

Love's not a candle; it's the freakin' sun.

Part 1

PEOPLE
WHO TAUGHT
ME LOVE

Chapter 1

MY FIRST LOVE (GUS)

There's nothing half so sweet in life as love's young dream.
—Thomas Moore

Do you remember your first love? What it taught you? Mine was my very first lesson in love without limits, and I was never the same.

My first love was Gus Tate,[1] whose swing set loosely separated my unfenced backyard from his in Peachtree City, Georgia. I was six years old; Gus was four. I was a girl; he was a boy. I was Lutheran; he was Catholic. I went to school; he stayed home. On the block, the kids teased, "Eww, he's too little to play with." At church, they said, "Eww, his church is bad and teaches the wrong stuff." For these silly reasons, everyone said Gus and I couldn't be best friends. Thankfully, we never let that stop us.

Gus and I spent hours together every day, our shared love for SpaghettiOs, playing outside, and the book *Bedknobs and Broomsticks* drowning out all the voices that tried to keep us apart. Gus's dad worked for a big company in Atlanta. He always left the house early, so we didn't see him much, just like my dad. Gus's mom, Margaret, was as sweet as could be, and, just like my mom, she fed us cut-up apple slices and Kool-Aid, but always with less sugar added than the back of the packet recommended. Unlike the rest of the world, Gus and I realized how much we had in common, which made our love as shatterproof as our sippy cups.

Gus and I turned up our noses at store-bought games, like Tiddlywinks or Cootie, in favor of our own invented game called Imagination, our favorite version of which we called Magic Carpet. The game required only a fuzzy blue bath mat and an old little tube, which although it said Crest on it actually should have said Magic (duh, grownups!). To play, Gus and I sat on the little carpet, and I unscrewed the cap off the tube. Next, we held hands and wished as hard as we could for lift-off. Once airborne, eyes closed, we imagined our way across the world. *Look, that's the roof of your house down there! This must be what Mary Poppins feels like!* I swear sometimes that bath mat really did lift a few inches off the linoleum.

When our carpet grew tired—or more likely, when Margaret said it was time for supper—we opened our eyes and landed. The tube always went back home with me in my pocket, but only until the next time Gus begged me to uncap it. And there was always a next time.

One sad day, I lost the tube. To our delight, Gus and I found that it made no difference. The only magic we needed to fly was each other.

Once, in the woods behind our backyards, we discovered a huge fire-ant pile. Margaret told us the true story of a toddler who stepped into a pile of Georgia fire ants and died of allergic shock. The story frightened me but also filled me with me with a sense of big-girl responsibility. I knew I had to protect Gus from the scary piles of red dirt, because underneath them lurked a thousand sneaky ants that could sting the life out of him in a second. Time with Gus taught me that you have to look out for everyone who is littler than yourself—and that protecting people from things that sting is what love looks like.

Even though I was only a little kid, Margaret loved and trusted me. Somehow, I knew this. I see now that I was in some ways a helpful babysitter to her during a tough time in her life, but that doesn't change a thing about my gratitude. Gus was kind and sweet, and he let me teach him stuff he didn't know how to do, like read books, tie his shoes, and brush his teeth. In my own family, I was the littlest, which felt like the stupidest. But with Gus, I felt smart and special. Gus was the first person in my life who made me feel like a someone, like the teacher I would one day become.

On what went down in my personal history as the worst day of my childhood, all of this goodness came to a wailing halt. A few weeks before my seventh birthday, Gus and Margaret moved to Kansas. I had no idea where Kansas was. But like every kid, I had watched *The Wizard of Oz*, so I knew Kansas was a nightmarish place—far from your family and filled with cyclones and mean green witches. I could not for the life of me understand why Gus had to go there. My mom said that Gus was moving because his parents had gotten a divorce. I had no idea what divorce was, but because it meant that Gus was leaving town forever and I could no longer walk out my back door and see his face, I rightly understood the "d" word to stand for separation, tears, and never again being able to play on the swing-set with the person I loved.

The day Gus left town, I stared out my window at the orange Allied moving van in its hearse-like hugeness. I cried the entire day. I couldn't stop. This continued for days. No one in my family paid me any attention. They all thought I would get over it. In one way, they were right. But in another way, they were dead wrong, as evidenced by the fact that I'm still sitting here writing about him decades later.

A month or so after Gus moved, I wrote him a letter on my yellow-lined monogrammed stationery, which he had sent me for my seventh birthday. I wrote, "I miss you so much Gus. I will never smile again," and I mailed it to him. This was overly dramatic, I know. But today I'm struck by how much this reaction foretold about my life and revealed who I really am deep down. Grief has always stung my soul like a thousand Georgia fire ants swarming my skin. It has always left me shocked, gasping for air, and terrified of dying all alone in the woods. I could lie to you and swear that one day I outgrew this allergic reaction to absence. But honestly, I never did. Like all grown-ups, I just learned how to hide it.

As you might imagine, my letter troubled Margaret. She (and Gus) wrote me back. Gus couldn't write yet, so she had to speak for him. "Jackie," she penned, "Gus was so sad to hear you say that you will never smile again. He wants you to play and be happy. He wants you to know that he will never forget you." I still have this letter. I have kept it for forty years.

I never saw Gus Tate again.

But for the next twenty years, we wrote letters. Each year I sent him my school picture, with my red-headed curly hair and my pale, freckled face smiling at him across the miles, proof that I had broken my grim promise. Gus sent me drawings, Valentines, a notice of his first Communion, school pictures. I grew up with my pictures of Gus on my bedroom desk, and I was told Gus grew up with pictures of me on his fridge. I always felt better when I heard this, because my greatest fear was that Gus would forget me. The saddest thing I could imagine was standing in my backyard all alone, the only one left holding the memory of how marvelous it felt to make lift-off.

As sometimes happens with time, the letters trickled to a slow drip, then stopped altogether. The very last thing Gus ever sent me, in the early '90s, was his wedding photo. Gus stood outside on the grass, in front of some lush green trees. He wore a tuxedo. I was struck by how much he looked like his dad.

However, what took my breath away in the photo was not Gus's face but the face of Gus's bride. She had red, curly hair and freckles all over her pale skin. Looking at the face of Gus Tate's wife felt like looking in a mirror. She looked more like me than my own sister.

Gus Tate is the person who taught me that real love never forgets—even if it has to move to Kansas, and you never, ever see it again. Gus Tate is the person who taught me that real love hurts you, but it also can heal you. A first love teaches you the power of certain things—magic, flight, stings, separation, words—and if you're one of the lucky ones, you'll never forget its lessons.

I am lucky. I never forgot.

At age six, I could never have known how divided our world, and even our own nation and neighborhoods, would one day become, how sad and severed. I could never have imagined the countless times I would hear someone say—or act as if—certain groups of "thems" or certain kinds of "theys" must never be loved or befriended because they were too different. I could never have foreseen how many times my heart would return to the memory of my minutes with Gus Tate, and how because of him and our magic, to this day I distrust voices that claim it's wrong or dangerous or unfaithful to love someone because they are not one of "us." I could never have fathomed the gratitude my grown-up self would still carry today for my childhood friend, for Gus Tate was the one who taught me to tear down the foolish fences this world tries to construct in my backyard. He was the one who taught me that, sure, differences and distance matter. But everyone—yes, everyone—wants to fly.

This is a book about love's legacy. About the likely and unlikely people, places, and things that have, in my years on earth, showed me how to love with a radical love. Always be ready to give an accounting of the hope that is within you, advises 1 Peter 3:15. This book is my heart on the page, giving you an accounting of the love that lives within me.

This is a book about love, love without limits. About the kind of outlandish love that outfoxes death, difference, and distance.

About all the people and places and things that you're taught not to love, and why loving them anyway might just save your life as well as stop the madness that currently passes for our daily news headlines. This is a book about a love so strong-legged, its leap crosses canyons. About a love so long-armed, its embrace makes room for you, and all your hidden grief too. About a challenge to widen love's wingspan, or die trying.

This is not a book about the tiny love fear teaches us to follow, fit for ants. It's about the goliath love God begs us to borrow, fit for giants. It's about the radical love to which we are called and the surprising places it will take us, if we are brave enough to believe— and hold hands.

Chapter 2

A MOTHER'S LOVE
(CHARLOTTE)

Watch and listen. You are the result of the love of thousands.
—Linda Hogan in *Dwellings: A Spiritual
History of the Living World*

Do not forsake your mother's teaching.
—Proverbs 6:20

Right after college, I spent a year teaching English in Japan. One afternoon, I ran a relay race with my middle-school students. They were elated that I was willing to put on shorts and sneakers and be their equal. When it was my turn, I ran my heart out on the dirt track. I didn't want to let them down. At the last second, I passed the sweat-soaked neon-orange baton to Kumiko. She fumbled and almost dropped it. Once she had it firmly in hand, she ran her heart out too. And so it went on down the line.

Love—in a world as tough as this one—is a relay race. If you're fortunate enough to ever clutch its baton in your hand, it's because someone passed it to you. And once you figure out how to hold it tight and run, someone waits at the other end with her hand outstretched.

Who are the people in your life who've taught you the most about love? The older I get, the more I realize that few things in life are more important than to figure out who those people are and then to carve out some serious time to look closely at the batons they've passed to you. If you're like me, doing so can lead to some much-needed self-reflection about the life you're living. Love—or the lack thereof—is the only legacy any of us leave behind.

Hands down, the person in my life who taught me the most about a love without limits was my mother. In biblical Hebrew the word for *compassion* comes from the word *womb*. In my life, this fits. My mother's womb gave birth not only to me but also to the love that lives within me.

My mother was a serious woman. When I was a kid, I believed she just didn't know how to chillax and have fun. As an adult, I finally recognize that her life resembled that of a hummingbird in a hurricane. My mother understood that while you were busy looking in the opposite direction, everything you once had could vanish. When she was six, she came home from school to find her entire house—along with all of her blankets, dolls, and books— burned to the ground. When she was fifteen, she discovered an old letter that her eighteen-wheeler-truck-driving dad had written to a relative a few days after she was born, and that scarred her sense of worth and lovability. In it her father wrote: "Today I made it to Kenosha, and Alice gave birth to a girl. I can't believe how late the thaw is coming this year; I'm so tired of all this snow on the road."

When my mom was eighteen and in her first semester of college, her dad died. When her mom asked her to drop out and come home to help take care of her two younger siblings, she did—and she never got to fulfill her dream of being the first in her family to graduate from college. When my mom was twenty, her brother was drafted into the Vietnam War. He survived, but with such crippling

PTSD that he went completely off the grid, rarely speaking to her or anyone else. When she was twenty-one, she got married; she hoped for tenderness, but instead got truculence. When she was twenty-three, her sister, niece, and nephew were in a terrible car accident that killed her infant nephew instantly and left her niece with permanent brain damage. When she was forty-seven, the last of her children—whom she had devoted all of her life to raising—emptied the nest, filling her soul with depression. And finally, when she was fifty, early onset Alzheimer's disease robbed her of all of her memories, which made every face in the entire world a stranger to her—but ironically erased all of the above from her mind. My sister and I once said that our mom might be the only person who ever got Alzheimer's and was relieved. We were wrong, of course, or so I want to believe.

The Bible says we love others because God first loved us (1 John 4:19). The Greek word used in this verse is *agape*. In the Greek language of biblical times, there were a lot of words used to mean love for particular groups of people—like *philia*, a love for one's friends; *eros*, a love for one's sexual partner; and *storge*, a love for one's family. Although most of us humans obsess every day over these kinds of love, scripture spends almost no time on them. Instead, whenever Jesus spoke of how he wanted us to love one another and himself, he used only one word: *agape*, the unconditional, universal love that God gifts to all people, all the time—no exceptions.

Love in Jesus' eyes was not how we think of it—like a table at a fancy restaurant with a RESERVED sign on it. Instead, it was something as wide-open as the sky itself. This was, and still is, radical. Here's a way to imagine it: we care about whether we get pumpernickel or white or wheat, but God cares only about bread itself—and making sure everyone has enough of it. *Agape* is Jesus' word to describe a new recipe for living: a love without limits.

In 1 John 4:19, *agape* is a verb. The verse actually says we *agape* others because God first *agape*-ed us. My mother's life testifies to the truth of this statement. Almost everyone—myself included—failed to love her as she deserved, but she *agape*-ed on anyway, with the woodcutting force of an adze. No one could be responsible for this other than God, whom my mother loved with quiet abandon. Her faith was the most reckless thing in her life.

I can't remember a time when my mother wasn't involved in the church. At one time she was the church librarian, at another the treasurer, and at all times, a choir member. One of my fondest young-adult memories was the sound of her steady voice next to mine in the choir, especially during our three back-to-back Christmas Eve services. My mother was a soprano, but she never sang a solo. The only time I ever heard her sing alone was in the afternoons after school, when I often caught her at the piano, practicing hymns from the green *Lutheran Book of Worship*. "Go Tell It on the Mountain," "Be Thou My Vision," and "Immortal Invisible" were her favorites.

We tracked the decline of my mother's Alzheimer's by her relationship to these hymns she cherished. When she forgot who she was, she still sang their lines. When she forgot the words, she hummed the notes. When she forgot how to hum, she whistled the tunes. When she forgot how to whistle, she smiled when we turned the radio on next to her bed. Music was the friend she never forgot.

We sang all three of my mom's favorite hymns at my wedding. Their melodies didn't exactly make me feel like my mom was there, but they did make me feel like she could've been peeking in through the stained-glass windows.

My mom didn't say "I love you" a lot. She wasn't an emotive person. But more than anyone in this world, she showed me what love looks like. Take mornings, for instance. My mother didn't believe in alarm clocks for other people (only for herself). She woke me up every single day for school, even when I was in high school, by gently saying my name from my bedroom doorway. She'd tell me the day's weather forecast (so I knew how to dress). Then she'd ask me what I wanted for breakfast (so that I'd have to wake up fully enough to respond).

By the time I made it to the kitchen, voila, my breakfast smiled up at me. The bowl of Marshmallow Krispies, the creamed chipped beef, the Eggo waffle, and on special days with tests or field trips, a fried egg on toast with cheese. Beside the plate stood two kid-sized jelly jars, one filled with water, the other juice. And if it was a cereal day, a third filled with milk for me to add myself (so my cereal wouldn't get soggy). Beside these sat a Flintstones chewable vitamin (so I didn't have to swallow a pill—terrifying!). Sometimes in my morning rush I would forget to take it. Eight hours later I'd come home from school, the kitchen spotless except for a purple Fred Flintstone, sweating in the middle of the table with his skin a shade darker than when I'd left. "You forgot to take your vitamin," my mom would say as I walked into the kitchen. "How was school?"

Wherever I pause the mental DVD of my childhood, my mother stands at the edge of every frame. Band concerts, PTA meetings, football game half-time shows, all-state music competitions—you name it, there she was. Growing up, I thought all mothers were like her. I was a fool.

One time in the first grade, I disobeyed my mom in a major-league way. As she did every morning during breakfast, my mother listened to the weather forecast on her AM radio. Bad storms were predicted. She told me to ride home on the school bus, rather than walk like I often did. I didn't listen. I walked home with my friend Kelly through the woods. A storm broke out. The rain spilled down in sheets. The thunder clapped over our heads. The Georgia red clay turned to pure mud. It stained my new white Keds and trapped Kelly's sandal. She fell down, scraping her knee on a stone. When we finally arrived at my back door, we were soaked, our tears indistinguishable from the rain. My mother was beside herself with worry. Madder at me than she had ever been before, she insisted we throw the rust-colored Keds away. Money was super tight at that time. Waste was wrong, and I was ashamed.

Later in life, I went on a church retreat. The leader asked us to write an apology letter to someone we had wronged, seeking their forgiveness. I wrote to my mom about the day I walked home through the storm. My mom, who possessed a perfectly fine memory at that time, called me on the phone. "Thank you for your letter," she said. "But I honestly don't remember that day at all."

Love, author Ray Bradbury once said, is to give people back to themselves, better than they ever hoped or dreamed. To this I can only respond, *preach, Ray Bradbury, preach.*

In the sixth grade, I won the school spelling bee. I had never been good at anything, especially not things involving trophies. I had never won anything either, unless you counted in kindergarten when I stumbled upon the golden egg in our city's Easter-egg hunt and won a basket of candy bigger than me. So when I won the bee, I was giddy with glee. I asked my mom how I could improve for the countywide competition. She suggested we start practicing before school.

So we started getting up every day, just the two of us, at 5:00 a.m. It was dark outside, and the crickets still sang their nighttime hymns to the stars. My mom found hard words in her two-volume *World Book* dictionary and asked me to spell them. "Exaggeration," she'd say. "Bauble." If I missed a word, the next morning she'd ask me that same one again.

I went on to win the entire county. I won a big blue trophy, a little black-and-white TV, and $300 in savings bonds. The local newspaper ran an article with the headline "Clay County Spelling Bee Champion" and a picture of me, standing at the microphone in a maroon bow tie. My mother clipped it out and put it in the top drawer of her antique pie safe, where she kept all her favorite secret stuff and where I found it years later.

SCHOOL BOARD MEMBER George Bush presents the 1983 Spelling Bee Championship Trophy to Jackie Bussie, 13-year-old Lakeside Middle School student who correctly spelled L-I-B-E-L and then went on to spell O-G-R-E to win the championship.

With more pre-dawn practice, I went on to the state bee. I placed third, one place shy of getting to go on to the big national spelling bee in Washington, DC. I misspelled the word *ptyxis*, a word my mother and I had never studied and that surprised us both with its silent *p*.

Losing sucks. Love—as badly as it longs to—doesn't always have the power to change outcomes. But win or lose, solidarity changes everything. This is what my mother's sweaty-vitamin-no-alarm-5:00-a.m.-wakeups taught me. I still think getting up early is beastly, but the sun would never beat me out of bed if I could wake up to that kind of solidarity again. Solidarity was the origami swan my mother made out of her papercut life.

My mom's batons have saved me more times than I can count. Especially in my relationship with my own faith, which, unlike my mother's, remains as rocky and slippery as a creek bed. Some-times—okay, well, loads of the time—I'm livid with God for stuff like kids with cancer, adults with Alzheimer's, tsunamis in Thai-land, and earthquakes in Ecuador. I can't fathom why God doesn't stop certain losses from happening. But sometimes I can check my anger by remembering what my mom must have admired so much in Jesus: his I'll-never-leave-your-side solidarity.

There was nowhere that sucked—prisons, slums, deserts, court-rooms, leper colonies, hell—where Jesus refused to go, as long as someone he loved was already there. When he could, Jesus freed people from their hells. When he couldn't, he linked arms with them and walked beside them on their road to Emmaus. At the end, he died alongside them, so no one would ever have to walk solo down that lonely street again.

Those of us who know what it feels like when love stays, know what a difference accompaniment makes. Jesus was the master of accompaniment. His song of solidarity, much like my mother's, showed the world how to transform the beastly into the bearable, even the beautiful. "I will not leave you as orphans, I am coming to you" (John 14:18).

My mother never spoke much about herself, or about her own dreams. Most of the things I know about her I had to find out from other people, or pry them out of her like a first responder dragging a child from the rubble. One day she let escape the fact that she had always dreamed of becoming a physical therapist, and ever since then, I've felt sad that her dream was never realized.

One afternoon, though, on the way home from school, I spot-ted her yellow Karmann Ghia in the church parking lot. I decided to stop in to see what she was doing, and I found her in the fel-lowship hall. A wheelchair sat in the middle of the room, next to a massage table. On the table was a child I'd never seen before—a child with severe disabilities. My mother was holding her ankles, and moving her skinny misshapen legs in a slow repetitive kick.

Off to the side sat a woman—I suppose the girl's mom—her head tilted back and eyes closed. My mom's back was to me. I watched her for a few minutes. She was totally absorbed.

Finally, she glanced back and noticed me. Her expression resembled that of a child caught eating cookies instead of carrots. "Serena's muscles atrophy if we don't help her move them for a few hours a day," she explained, without ever stopping the motion of her arms. I never knew my mother did anything like this. She had never once mentioned it. I had no idea how long she'd been doing this, or how often, or how she'd ever even met these people. It made me wonder how many other things about my mom I didn't know. It made me hope, suddenly, that there were a lot.

Toward the end of high school, I told my mom that my dream was to go to college, in spite of my family's rule: "Women don't need to go to college." While I was growing up, this actual sentence was said to me more times than I'd like to remember (though never by my mother). My older sister accepted this advice and didn't go. But I resisted. I loved school more than anything.

I awoke late one night in my senior year of high school to hear my mom in an argument. "Jacquie's the valedictorian of her class. She needs to go to college," I heard her say heatedly. In my family, this may be the only argument my mother ever won. If lives swing on hinges, here's where mine swung up and out. If all the angels in heaven did me a solid, strapped on jetpacks, and painted *THANK YOU, MOM* across the entire sky in puffy white contrails, the letters still wouldn't match their height in my heart.

When I finally made it to college, my mom sent me care packages. They were filled with all the little things I liked best—packs of HARIBO gummy bears, yellow boxes of golden raisins, honeysuckle-scented anything, Finesse shampoo, and once, a six-pack of Cherry 7Up. These packages were hilarious to the other girls in my dorm. "Girl, surely you can go buy your own Finesse shampoo at Walgreens!" they would tease. Of course they were right.

But they didn't know what I knew. For my mother, care packages were what love looked like, wearing stamps and your name on the address line.

My mom's *agape*-ing extended beyond human beings and encircled creation with its wide arms. When we used to go for walks through our neighborhood after dinner, she always tucked a plastic Winn-Dixie grocery bag in her pocket. Whenever she saw a piece of trash on the walk, she'd stop, pick it up, and throw it in the bag. This embarrassed me, and I feared the eyeballs of the neighborhood kids. (This was the '80s, remember, when going green was definitely *not* a thing.) One evening, I whined about how my mom kept stopping on our walk to pick up dirty Snickers wrappers and Budweiser cans that weren't even ours. She replied, "Fences are liars." In her mind, all of creation was her backyard.

One day, my mom and I were driving home from my clarinet lesson. As we turned a familiar corner, she gasped. She pulled over the car, and I asked her what was wrong. She pointed shakily to the spot where, for my entire childhood, a plot of lush woods had stood. A bulldozer gored into the trunks of the remaining live oaks in front of a developer's sign. We sat by the side of the road for at least ten minutes—the time it took for my mother to stop sobbing.

When I was a kid, my mom always said, "I want you to know that fruits and vegetables don't come from a grocery store." And off we'd go, driving hours to U-Pick farms where we'd harvest blueberries, strawberries, and other fruits while we contemplated soil, seeds, and hands. My favorites were always the peaches—the ones we picked during the summers in Georgia. My mother taught me: you've never tasted a peach until you've climbed the ladder, braved the bees, stuck your hand in the heavy boughs, and plucked for yourself. Also: a peach is ready when its colors perfectly match the sunset. To this day, I remember exactly how delicious those peaches tasted, how sticky the ripe sunset felt as it dripped down my chin.

I'm a person who lost my mother not once, but twice. First to Alzheimer's, then to death. But, as you can tell, my memory of the things she taught me lives on, as strong and scenty and sweet as the taste of a summer Georgia peach.

These days, writing is how I metabolize life and its losses and break them down into useable nutrition. I learned this idea from the writer Julia Cameron, who urges us to metabolize our injuries into art.[1] Putting pen to paper is one of my favorite forms of prayer. Whenever I write, I pray to be the straw through which wisdom from God and other people flows.[2] If my mother Charlotte were here, I know she'd have a lot more she would want to share with you about love. So yesterday, I prayed that my pen would flow with what she might want me to tell you. Here's how that prayer was answered.

Charlotte's Forty Love Lessons

1. Even if you are not a great singer, sing anyway. God will love the sound of your voice, simply because it is yours.
2. If it gets to be too much inside, go outside. The sun on your face feels like an "I'm sorry" from the world, or from God.
3. Always visit sick, old, dying, and hurting people. Most people avoid looking hardship in the face, but you must always sit down beside it and look it straight in the eye.
4. Everyone just wants to be loved. It's always within your power to give this to people, even when you don't feel it yourself.
5. Even if you didn't get to have/see/do it, you can still create a world in which your children might.
6. Always put a little lipstick on in the car at the first red light. Smiles need to be seen.
7. If you make a promise, keep it. Forever is forever, even if it hurts.

8. Never lend money, but instead give it away—especially to those who have less than you. The love of money is a slave trader who will auction off the souls of the people you love.

9. Showing a person that you remember what they love is how you love them.

10. Grow something—roses, tomatoes, a child. Growing whatever you can helps sadness sprout a parachute so it descends slower upon the afternoon.

11. We are our wounds—but we can be so much more than them.

12. When on vacation, eat pie for breakfast. You might never have another chance.

13. If someday I forget everything, even myself, love asks you to remember me.

14. Cherish old things. Antiques bear the price tag of someone's memories. This goes for people as well as things.

15. Enjoy the company of older folks. You might not make it to be their age, and if not, now is the only moment you have to learn from them.

16. Love means feeding other people day after day, even when they don't say thank you.

17. Go to church. Church is where, unlike in your own house, hymns happen. Church is where, unlike in your own house, you are trusted with the money and the books.

18. Talk to your plants as you would your kids. Your breath helps them grow.

19. It is possible to give birth to a child you will feel, one day, like you do not know at all. If, God forbid, this happens to you, know you are not alone.

20. Love other people the way you have never been loved by them.

21. It is always worth getting up at 5:00 a.m. and driving forty-five minutes to the beach, because the sunrise needs a

witness. If the sun can climb back up on its feet to fight the storms and smog for one more day, so can you.

22. Getting up early feels good and is the only time your house feels like yours.

23. Never fall asleep until the last person you love finally comes home.

24. Mothers are the world's best cheerleaders.

25. Make it your goal every day to make everyone around you feel comfortable in their own skin.

26. Tuck a special note in your child's lunch box—"Have a great day at school! Love you, Mom." Best. Portable. Dessert. EVER.

27. Don't reward your children's good grades with money or celebration. Good work is its own reward.

28. Love your body and listen to it. On vacation and weekends, let children sleep as late as their bodies need. The body never lies.

29. As hard as you try, sometimes in life it is not possible to get close to your parents, or even to know them. Avoid blame.

30. Do your best to love where you live. But forgive yourself if sometimes you have to head south.

31. A mother's work is never done.

32. Let your child choose to play the instrument she wants. Tell her only after she has decided on the clarinet for herself that you used to play it too.

33. Even if your own wings don't work, you can still teach your child to fly. This is the definition of *miracle*.

34. If you go on vacation and while you are gone your lawyer-neighbor steals the sapling that you just planted in your backyard and plants it in his own, don't get mad. Instead, plant roses along the fence that divides your lawn from his. In time, their buds will grow so thick you will no longer have to look upon what you lost.

35. Beauty and kindness are the best revenge (see #34).
36. Grow a garden; it can teach you how to live. There are three secrets to gardening. One, a patient yearning for color. Two, a desire to catch the earth being good. And three, a relentless belief in transformation.
37. Value your education. Being a student is the greatest privilege you will ever have. Not all are so lucky.
38. When in doubt, sing hymns.
39. When all is said and done, faith in God is the only safe hand to bet the entire kitty on.
40. Wear other people's joy like a fine fur. Nothing looks more beautiful on you.

Chapter 3

WHEN YOUR FRIENDS BECOME YOUR FAMILY (FRAMILY)

If we are to have peace on earth, our loyalties must become ecumenical rather than sectional. Our loyalties must transcend our race, our tribe, our class, and our nation. . . . We must either learn to live together as brothers [and sisters] or we are all going to perish together as fools.
—Rev. Martin Luther King Jr.[1]

When I was a little kid, we had a beloved cat named Smokey. Smokey loved to hunt anything that moved. Whenever he caught something he was proud of—a field mouse, a chameleon— he dragged it with his little teeth all the way to our front door and then yowled like a banshee. The first time I saw Smokey do this I was totally weirded out because I didn't know what he wanted. But after Mom explained it to me and my siblings, we all understood. What Smokey was doing was totally natural. Like a kid bringing a drawing home from school to show his parents, Smokey just wanted to show us his prized handiwork. From then on, whoever answered the door always exclaimed "Oh, good kitty!! Great job,

Smokey!" After we praised him a few times, he'd strut away with his gray tail sticking straight up, like a flag atop a mountain.

Let's just say that after the loss of my mother in my twenties, I became Smokey, but with a major difference. Nothing I did earned me a "good kitty!" from the people inside my house. Nobody intended me harm, as far as I can tell. Perhaps they were too busy to answer the door, or perhaps, like me when I was younger, they simply didn't understand that that was what I needed.

In my family, I'm the first woman to go to college, and the first person ever to go to graduate school, let alone get a PhD. Working full-time in addition to school, I took seven years to finish my doctorate in theology and religion. In Smokey's terms, my PhD diploma was the mother lode of mouse catches. But on the day I graduated, not a single one of my family members came to see me get my diploma or even called to say congratulations. Of course, many of them had perfectly good reasons why they couldn't make it. My father, though, emailed late the night before to say he wasn't going to make it, no reason or apology given. I almost missed his email on the way out the door to go pick him up at the airport.

Take any religious, political, or social issue you can imagine, and my entire family disagrees with me on it. I know I'm not the only one for whom this is true. Some of us are misfits in our families of origin. You know how sometimes the laundry gets sorted and stuff ends up in the wrong drawer? Let's just say, I'm definitely a sock who landed up in with the sweaters.

I wish I could promise you that it all turns out okay in the end. But honestly, I don't know. All our culture's clichés—*Family is life's greatest blessing! Family is where life begins and love never ends!*—shout that loving our family should be easy-peasy. But for many of us, our bio-families push our ability to love to the limit. For a long time I was totally ashamed of this. I saw my misfit status and my tough relationship with my own family as an embarrassment, a liability. Though I still wish things were different, at last I've come to see all those early years living with my bio-family as something else: a top-notch training ground for love across difference. A gym for strengthening love's hamstrings to the level where they can leap beyond bloodlines or biology. That's how high God ultimately wants our love to launch, anyway, so why not start early?

Now, I'm *not* saying that if you get along famously with your family, you can't learn to love like that (of course you can, people do it all the time). I'm just saying that if you're someone who *doesn't*, there's an unrecognized upshot: you have a head start. You have a home gym, while others have to leave their living room to go work out. Of course, none of this changes the fact that some days you'd rather not work out at all.

During the long, hard years when my mother forgot who I was, I began to turn outward. I started letting myself love—and be loved by—people outside my family of origin. My friends, students, professors, and colleagues became the family grace created around me. I called (and still call) these beautiful humans my friend-family, or for short, my framily. I want you to meet some of them, because they've taught me a crazy lot about love without limits.

Meet My Framily

While I was in college, I met Dr. Tony Abbott in a required college course. He quickly became a favorite professor and lifelong mentor. Fifteen years after I graduated, Tony's wife, Susan, threw him a massive seventieth birthday party. I had secretly thought of Tony as a father figure since I was seventeen, though I was too afraid to tell him so. Tony said that this big birthday party was like the wedding party he and his wife never got to host. You see, Tony's only daughter died when she was four years old, so she didn't live to get married. And me, well, I'd felt parentless for a long, long time. I had never really known what Tony thought about me or what role I played in his life. At his birthday party, however, he stood up and introduced me to everyone there as his adopted daughter. My heart sang like Orphan Annie's.

Because of Tony, I went on to become a professor myself. Several years into my teaching, I was in a terrible car accident that resulted in a back injury. As part of my physical therapy, the doctor instructed me to go for frequent walks. But the pain made it hard to follow this advice without help. My husband was out of town for work at that time, so my students decided to take charge. More times than I can count, they showed up at my door to walk with me. I remember one evening on our walk, my student's girlfriend called him on his cell phone. I don't know exactly what she asked, but I heard him answer, "I'm sorry, but I can't right now. I'm walking my professor."

I laughed. And after our walk, I wrote in my journal: *People who love are like flower girls at a wedding. Lavishly they toss petals of time on to your path, not caring that they emptied their basket in celebration of you.*

And meet Liz, a friend who attended my wedding in 2003. When my husband and I were unwrapping our wedding gifts, we came across Liz's. It wasn't like the others, fancy and glittery—it was an old shoebox. I lifted off the lid. Inside were lots of little treats—honeysuckle candles, my favorite scent; Sun-Maid raisins in little yellow boxes; Nutri-Grain bars; cinnamon Pop-Tarts; a bag of Skittles; a bag of HARIBO gummy bears; and a small bowl bearing the sticker "Charlotte's Place." After a second, I grasped what this gift was, then tears—oh so many. Liz lived in my dorm during my early college years. She knew my mother, Charlotte, and her college care packages. Even more, Liz knew that for a bride who missed her mom like crazy on her wedding day, no present was more perfect than a gift of presence.

And then there's Matt, my lifelong best friend. We met in high school, when I was fourteen. My mother adored him. One summer when my mom was sick and I was caregiving, Matt came to visit. I asked him to stay with mom while I ran to the grocery store. When I got home, I heard "Rock Around the Clock" blasting from one of my dad's only-for-looks antique radios. I walked into the kitchen. Matt and my mom were dancing so hard they didn't see me. He was twirling my mother in his arms. Her smile was bigger than any sickness. I stood in the doorway and watched them, silently wishing for the song to never stop. If love-memories were the currency by which we gauged one another's wealth—as would be the case if this world had its values in order—this one made me the stunned owner of a mansion in Beverly Hills.

In my younger years, though, my mom's love for Matt often drove me to irritation. Once in high school, Matt brought his girlfriend to my house (while on a date!); I was furious. (Even then, I was already in love with him, but what teen would admit that?) My mother shocked me by defending him.

"Matt obviously has a crush on you," she deciphered. "Can't you see he does these silly things because you're more important to him than his girlfriends? If he ever stops talking to you about them, *then* you'll really have something to be upset about."

"Mom, whose side are you on, anyway!?!" I hollered back. Secretly, of course, I hoped she was right.

She was. Though my mom would never witness it, nineteen years after we met, Matt and I got married.

When I lost my mom, I truly believed that no one could ever love me like she did. You know, with that kind of love that scores an eleven on a scale of one to ten. This fear bit me like a rattlesnake, releasing a venomous recurring dream into my bloodstream.

In the dream, I'm living alone in a strange town, and I'm starving. Everyone else in the dream is eating lunch at big picnic tables. I've forgotten my lunch or lost it. When I sit down next to the townspeople and their brown paper bags, everyone is mean. They won't share any of their food or juice boxes with me. Alone, I wander into the woods. In a strange thicket, I come upon a woman working in front of a wood cabinet. She is wearing the red shorts/ red-and-white-striped shirt combo that my mom always loved to wear in the summertime. "Mom?" I say (I'm incredulous—isn't she dead?). The woman turns around. It's her. The sight of her kind eyes causes ten years of tears to roll down my face.

"Mom," I wail, "No one will share their lunch with me!"

"What? No lunch?" she asks, her voice calm and compassionate. She motions for me to sit down at her little picnic table. She makes me one of those ham-and-cheese-loaf sandwiches I loved as a kid, with the little flecks of cheese cross-stitched in the ham (I'm incredulous again—didn't Oscar Mayer stop making that stuff years ago?). I pick up the sandwich in both hands. Before I can take a bite, the sound of my own sobs wakes me up.

This recurring dream contained fear as raw as a fresh-cracked egg. The fear that I lived in a world where love had lost its way to my plate. Though it took me far too long to realize it, this fear was unfounded. Of course no one will ever, ever replace my mom, and I will miss her forever. But I do still have eleven-out-of-ten love in my life. My husband has given me that love back, in a hundred small ways, on a thousand different days.

One of the ways Matt salts my life with *agape* is by serving as house chef. Some days he carves hearts out of carrots and puts them on my salad. A lot of Saturdays he writes *I Love You* in Sriracha sauce on my omelet and serves it to me in bed.

I'm embarrassed to admit it, but until I sat here typing this, I never made the connection between my *What-no-lunch?* dream and Matt's lovingly prepared meals. I believe in redemption, but sometimes I have a really hard time seeing its edges. Life writes its own poetry, but like all poetry, it's sometimes hard to read.

So if you've been let down or wounded time and time again by your family of origin, know you're not alone. Let grace's nimble fingers weave a new family around you out of the silken thread of your friends. Refuse to sign for the package of shame and guilt society will FedEx you in response. Sometimes family has nothing to do with DNA.

Jesus' Framily Values

One of the main reasons Christians can embrace our framily—and beyond—is Jesus. Jesus' definition of family is radical and shocking; it's completely disconnected from biology. Take, for example, the time Jesus was addressing the crowd and someone said his mother and brothers were waiting outside to talk to him (Matthew 12:46). "But to the one who had told him this," Jesus replied, "Who is my mother, and who are my brothers?" And pointing to his disciples, he said, "Here are my mother and my brothers! For whoever does the will of my Father in heaven is my brother and sister and mother" (Matthew 12:48–50).

We often think of our biological family as our inner circle, which leaves everyone else standing outside waiting to get in. But Jesus reverses this. His point is clear: like a broth made from just one bean, our typical definition of family is too weak to work with.

Jesus declares: "If anyone comes to me and does not hate his father and mother, his wife and children, his brother and sisters— yes, even his own life, he cannot be my disciple" (Luke 14:26). I've rarely heard a sermon preached on this hate-your-family passage. The one time I did, the pastor explained that you have to love God more than anything, even your own family. In a world of competing loyalties, God has to win. It's a common interpretation, but I believe Jesus is trying to say something more.

A lot of folks are hopeful that this verse contains some kind of mistranslation, that the ancient word Jesus speaks here didn't really mean *hate*. Sorry, no capful of Downy can soften this one. The Greek word here—*miseo*—means to despise or to hate or, by extension, to love less. *Miseo* is used about forty times in the New Testament, and each time it gets translated as *hate*, as in Hebrews

1:9, "You have loved righteousness and hated wickedness, therefore God . . . has anointed you."

Elsewhere, as in 1 John 4:20, Jesus instructs us to love our brothers and sisters, which seems to contradict his words in Luke that we should hate those same folks. What's the deal? Is Jesus actually asking us to despise our parents, siblings, spouses, and kids? To find out, we need to take a look at the full context of Luke 14, arguably one of the most eye-popping chapters ever written on radical *agape*-love.

At the beginning of Luke 14, Jesus gets invited to a Sabbath dinner at the house of some Pharisees, those religious by-the-book elites who constantly get on Jesus' case for breaking rules. On the way there, Jesus sees a man with dropsy, what we nowadays call edema (Luke 14:2). Edema is an excess accumulation of fluid that causes painful, abnormal swelling; it disfigures parts of sufferer's bodies beyond recognition. Jesus heals this sick man, even though working on the Sabbath is against his religious tradition's laws. The religious folks observe Jesus' act in silent judgment. Sensing their hostility, Jesus defends himself, "If one of you has a child or an ox that falls into a well, will you not immediately pull it out on a Sabbath day?" (14:5). No one answers, because their egos won't let them admit Jesus is right: "And they could not reply to this" (14:6).

In this scene, Jesus busts boundaries. Brilliantly and boldly. Of course everyone would save a member of their own family no matter what freakin' day of the week it was. That's a no-brainer. But Jesus hasn't healed a member of his family. He's healed a total "stranger"—not only that, a stranger with an impure, unsightly illness that made most people run away in disgust. Jesus' action poses the question, If you would break the Sabbath to save your own kin, why not break it to save someone else's? He takes the people's respectable love of "their own"—their own family, their own animals—and bloats that category out to include folks never before admitted.

Jesus' scandalous healing swells the notion of family beyond recognition. You can almost hear the people around him thinking, "Wait, *those people* aren't my responsibility . . . are they?" Jesus' *agape* is excessive and abnormal; it painfully enlarges their circle of concern. It's no coincidence the man Jesus healed had edema. In healing him, Jesus gave love its own case of edema. Unsurprisingly, those around him wanted to run far away.

Continuing on in Luke 14, once at the Pharisee's house, Jesus sees guests vying for the best dinner seats near their powerful host. This prompts him to tell two parables. The first Jesus directs toward his host: "When you give a luncheon or a dinner, do not invite your friends or your brothers or your relatives or rich neighbors. . . . But when you give a banquet, invite the poor, the crippled, the lame, and the blind" (Luke 14:12–13). In the parable that follows, Jesus speaks to the guests: A wealthy man throws a massive dinner party. All the people he invites, however, have an excuse for why they can't make it. Work. Shopping. Time with "family." The usual. The guy then says to his servant, "Go out at once into the streets . . . and bring in the poor, the crippled, the blind, and the lame. . . . For I tell you, none of those who were invited will taste my dinner" (Luke 14:21–24).

Once again, as when he healed the man with edema, with these instructions Jesus swells love to the point of scandal. Jesus knows exactly what kind of people we are. Left to our own devices, we'll only love people who look, love, dress, worship, and work exactly like ourselves. As hosts, we'll invite and feed only those we know and love best, our relatives and best friends. But throwing a party for your own squad is, well, just that. How would your family react if you brought over all the local homeless folks for supper? Jesus asks us to invite over all those we fear and spurn for caviar and Dom Pérignon.

Jesus' *agape* is what my seminary professors called *superabundant*. Jesus schmears love around so liberally that it reminds me of the way my dad slabbed peanut butter on our toast when my mom wasn't home. So thick, it was borderline obscene. Also, tough to swallow. But for those brave enough to try a bite, wow—off the charts sensational.

By telling all these stories in Luke 14, Jesus tries to drive home one grand-slam message: *the way we love is absurdly too small.* Too selfish. Too limited. Too filled with exceptions. Our love is tiny; Jesus' is titanic. To follow Jesus, then, means to let God transform our love from tiny to titanic. In a nutshell, here's Jesus' advice when it comes to love: *Go big or go home, people.*

How will you know when your *agape*-love is as thick and wide and titanic as God wants? Well, if Jesus' own life is any indication, once you completely offend other people. Jesus wants us to distend our love so far, its swollen face will completely scandalize the VIPs, government officials, members of our own family, and especially the most powerful people within our own religious tradition. After all, that's what Jesus got for the way he loved. "If the world hates you, be aware that it hated me before it hated you" (John 15:18). Basically, if you annoy the heck out of the powerful, then you will know that your love has dilated sufficiently. Only dilated love can give birth to new life.

Next up in Luke 14 comes Jesus' speech that begins with hating your father and mother. After it, comes this: "Now all the tax collectors and sinners were coming near to listen to him. And the Pharisees and the scribes were grumbling and saying, 'This fellow welcomes sinners and eats with them'" (Luke 15:1–2). Do people say this about you? Do people think you keep good company or so-called bad company? Would people say you hang out with "those people" or with the "right" people? Jesus wants each one of us to ask ourselves these questions.

Now, in context, we can better understand Jesus' unusual advice to hate our immediate family. Because Jesus' bold words are sandwiched between incidents where people judge him for ballooning his love past "acceptable" boundaries, we know that these words also demand that we balloon *our* love out past acceptable boundaries. Those boundaries of acceptability need to be bulldozed, because God didn't build them—human beings did. Jesus, when he tells us to hate our families, challenges us to stretch our notion of *family* wider than we have ever done before. To love other people, such as "strangers," as much as we love our own families may very well feel like "hate" to those within our biological families, because they're used to getting the special red-carpet treatment reserved only for them. Consider the following scenario.

I have an acquaintance whose husband died on 9/11. A firefighter, he went into the second tower after the first had already collapsed. His loved ones assume he knew he probably wouldn't make it out alive. Still, he went in. To the world, he was nothing but a hero. But for his wife who had a new baby at home, things were more complicated. At the head level, she knew he was a hero and that what he did was the most loving, generous thing anyone could ever do for someone else. This huge-heartedness was, after all, one of the reasons she had fallen in love with him. But at the heart level, she struggled something fierce. Her husband had made a choice, and the choice was not her or their baby son. While she would not have used the word *hate* to describe what this felt like, some small part of her—not the whole, just a part—struggled against the feeling that her husband had loved those strangers more than he had loved his own family. And that was extremely painful. This, I believe, is the figurative sense of *miseo*, which the Greek dictionary defines as "to love less." Experiencing *hate* is often the sensation of feeling loved less.

I know I would've felt the exact same way as the firefighter's widow, which raises in my mind a troubling but important question when it comes to God. Am I okay with God loving me as much as God loves other people? No. Secretly, or even unconsciously, I want God to love me *more*. Luke 14 suggests that a lot of what I experience as pain and suffering results from one thing: God loving someone else as much as God loves me. Ouch. I may say I want a love without limits, but when I search my heart of hearts, I find I really prefer an exclusive love, a love that favors me and the things I want.

What if what *feels* to some like being loved less, both by God and by others, really isn't? What if it's actually being loved *as much as* someone else? And what if what privileged people like me call hate sometimes is nothing more than a loss of top-dog status? Sometimes honest answers to hard questions like these unlock doors we didn't even know were deadbolted.

Consider, for example, Black Lives Matter (BLM). On the news, I saw a white man spitting rage at the movement. He, like many white folks, called BLM a hate group. Luke 14—and its hard questions—came bounding into my brain with a fury. Also the poster my students of color gave me that says,

> WHEN YOU'RE ACCUSTOMED TO PRIVILEGE,
> EQUALITY FEELS LIKE OPPRESSION.

I hung that poster on my wall so that as a white person I wouldn't forget its message, which pretty much dovetails with Jesus' own. In a world as tough as this one, feeling loved and being told you matter is a privilege. It sure as hell shouldn't be, but it is.

When grown men in my family told me I had no right to go to college simply because God made me a girl, it stung like nothing else. In response, I resisted. I protested with my entire life. I not only went to college, I never left (I became a college professor). I would be a total hypocrite if I ever forgot how much being treated as less-than sucked.

In nearly all other ways in my life, however, I've been treated as a beloved child of God. Because my skin is white, society has told me that I matter. When I listen to some of my friends of color talk about their lives and how they've been treated, I can't help but see that what is true for me is not true for everyone. When I see members of Black Lives Matter through God's lens of radical love, I can do nothing other than stand arm-in-arm with them.

Being told we're less-than is waste unless we compost the experience and widen the wingspan of our love to include people who're being told the exact same thing.

When Jesus says we have to hate our mothers and fathers, sisters and brothers, he means that we have to live in a way that shows the world: your true family is infinitely more than members of your own clan, nation, race, sexuality, tax bracket, or religion. It's everyone. This sounds like a warm fuzzy in the abstract, but just try living it out. The world will perceive loving this way as strange, if not totally irresponsible and disloyal. Like running back into a burning building to save a kid who's not your own, while your own kid stands on the curb begging you not to leave him. Ouch.

Many people in the world—especially those used to the biggest slice of love's pie—don't even recognize radical love as love at all, but instead as a disfigurement of love's face. Jesus' use of the extreme word *hate* captures how alien God's all-embracing *agape* feels to those who do not yet comprehend a love that excludes no one from the shelter of its sky.

Equality is a painful thing for those accustomed to not having to share, even when the thing we're talking about sharing is love. Capacious canopy love is terrifying and baffling. Human nature panics. We assume there is *not* enough love to go around.

I once received a lovely handwritten card from a new coworker. Later, I learned that this generous person gives everyone cards, for every possible reason. When I learned this, I didn't feel special anymore. My ego tried to stage a coup against my happiness. It lost, thankfully. The secret to happiness is realizing that, like oxygen, there's enough to go around, and more gets made every day.

Love is the same. Love is like galaxies, not gasoline. It's not some precious resource that'll be sucked dry in twenty years, or an endangered species like the northern hairy-nosed wombat. Sometimes when I feel myself getting envious of a friend or a colleague, I actually repeat to myself like a mantra: *Jacqueline, there is enough love to go around.* Some of us need reminding.

God is basically my awesome card-giving colleague on steroids. But deep down how does that make us feel? A love that ensconces hundreds, millions, or billions often makes us feel insignificant or un-special. Exclusive love = sexy! ☺ Capacious love = totally unsexy. ☹ Who doesn't long to feel chosen and special? Maybe this is why Christians are so quick to decide who's out and who's in, who's "us" and who's "them," and why Jesus has to keep repeating like an exhausted mom: *Please stop already. How many times do I have to ask you?* Look closely at the word *exclusive*. Uh-oh. The problem with exclusive love? It *excludes*.

The gospel is not Wall Street. The two should never be confused. We quantify and commodify everything, but love wildly refuses to adhere to our market economics of scarcity. The more there is of it, the more it multiplies. *Agape* is like algae, not amethysts. Like mosquitoes, not money. Algae? Mosquitoes? See, I told you. Definitely unsexy.

God wrote the truth about love on the pages of the universe, but we keep missing the memo. Think, for example, of how the universe is constantly expanding. It balloons bigger with every passing second, which sounds terrifyingly like something that would annihilate us. Turns out, though, it's exactly the perfect pace for everyone to thrive. The universe whispers: *love like this.*

Saint Augustine once wrote, "God loves each one of us as if there were only one of us." Again, preposterous. How can any one love do this for seven billion people? I can't explain it, but I think I've seen it. Have you ever walked or run beside an ocean or lake as the sun rests low in the sky over the water? Next time you do, notice how the sun's light blazes a path from the sky straight to your feet. Walk parallel to the water's edge, and watch—the beam follows you like a spotlight. But that's not even the best part. Though it appears that the glow glints alongside you and you only, the truth is, in that exact same moment, everyone else beside the water sees the sun gallop alongside them as if *they* were the only one. This is God's *agape* message in a bottle, written in sunlight ink.

"The problem with humanity is that we draw the circle of our family too small," Mother Teresa once said. To test her quote, recently in my theology class I asked my students to draw their families. Only "immediate" relatives made the Crayola cut. They drew their families almost exactly as I had when I was in kindergarten—parents, siblings, pets.

We then read Luke 14 aloud. I asked my students to turn their papers over, and draw their families as Jesus defines them.

These sketches on the pages' flip side blew my mind—they were completely different than the initial ones. One student drew a circle and wrote the word *everyone* inside it. Another drew the entire earth with holding-hands stick figures encircling it. How different would the world look if we really adopted Jesus' understanding of family?

As my husband likes to say, family is not the room you're born into, it's the room you walk into.

And as I like to say, every day I go out into the world as a loved person, and that changes everything. It's true in my case that the people who most often make me feel this way are not my biofamily. But Jesus gets that; it's part of the point he's making in Luke 14. Lovelines, not bloodlines, matter most.

The Apostle Paul: Christians Are Framily

According to the apostle Paul, a Christian understanding of family is based not on biology but on adoption. He writes, "For all who are led by the Spirit of God are children of God. For you . . . have received a spirit of adoption. When we cry, 'Abba! Father!' It is that very Spirit bearing witness with our spirit that we are children of God" (Romans 8:14–16). And to the Ephesians he writes, "Blessed be the God and Father of our Lord Jesus Christ, who has blessed us in Christ with every spiritual blessing. . . . He destined us for adoption as his children through Jesus Christ" (1:3–5).

Paul insists that although Christians worship the God of Abraham, they are not literal biological descendants of Abraham, "For not all who are descended from Israel are Israel. Nor because they are his descendants are they all Abraham's children. . . . In other words, it is not the natural children who are God's children but it is the children of the promise who are regarded as Abraham's offspring" (Romans 9:6–8). According to Paul, our Jewish brothers and sisters are God's "natural" children; Christians are only "grafted in."

While scripture views adoption as God's radical *agape* at its finest, we tend to see it as somehow second best, or not even real. Think of our language. One of my close friends was adopted by her aunt, who was the only mother she ever knew and an amazing one at that. But folks always ask her, "Do you know who your *real* mother is?" My friend answers by gesturing to her aunt in the kitchen, "I sure do—she's standing right there."

The Greek term that Paul uses for adoption—*huiothesia*—is a fascinating word. It's a combination of *huios*, meaning *descendant* or *son*, and a derivative of the word *theo*, meaning *God*—or, intriguingly, *to place in a horizontal position*. *Huiothesia*, or adoption, is how God makes us divine descendants. But the word's origins also suggest that God's family is horizontal rather than vertical. God's broad family traces its lineage not by blood, extending upward like a tree trunk, but by decision, extending outward like tree branches. In Jesus, God reaches out horizontally, as one of us, and draws us in to a family of infinite embrace.

This changes how we understand Communion, the Christian shared meal of the bread and the wine. To be honest, the ritual's repetition of Jesus' words, "My blood shed for you and for all people," has always troubled me, for what does that really mean, *to drink Jesus' blood*? We often assume it's about sacrifice and pouring out blood to appease a vengeful God. But I have come to believe that it's about something else.

As humans we're obsessed with blood and bloodlines. Many of the ugliest things we've ever done to one another were motivated by the desire to keep our blood "pure" and "uncontaminated" by others. Consider the Nazi hatred for people of "Jewish blood," or the widespread discrimination against people with HIV/AIDS. Consider also the racist US miscegenation laws that made it illegal until 1967 for African Americans and whites to intermarry; *miscegenation* is a Latin word that literally means *mixing of the families*. Blood has long been our idol.

To counter all of this horrible hatefulness, Jesus uses the symbolic meal of Communion. Every sip of the wine contains a lesson: the same blood runs through everyone's veins. As we drink down this truth, we share in Jesus' bloodline and become one family: the human family. Communion shares the same doormat as Luke 14. It sits at the entrance to God's home and reads:

WELCOME TO MY FAMILY;
YOU ARE NOW ALL RELATED.

Of course, we are a broken people who like to jigsaw apart this wholeness. This is why God insists that we share the bread and wine not once but over and over again. We need constant reminding that our sense of who is our "blood" and "flesh of our flesh" is too narrow, too vertical, too ancestry.com.

Our sense of family needs to be a circle and not a line, and that circle needs to be ever-widening. For many people, their framily is the first circle out from the center, and thus a necessary first step.

In order to live into the call to radical *agape*, Christians today need to reimagine and redefine family. Our new vision must broaden love's bandwidth. It must push back against culture's definition and instead align with Jesus' own. Our new vision of family must mushroom out to include all God's children. No asterisks, no disclaimers, no clauses, no provisions, no exceptions. Period.

Joseph and His Amazing Technicolor Framily

In the end, what does a love without limits have to say to all of us misfits? When read with fresh eyes, the biblical story of Joseph provides a clue.

By any account, Joseph's bio-family sucks. In today's terms, they're human traffickers. Joseph's own brothers are so jealous of his dreams and his father's gift to him of a coat of many colors that they sell him into slavery. "So Joseph went after his brothers, and found them at Dothan. They saw him from a distance, and before he came near to them, they conspired to kill him. They said to one another, 'Here comes this dreamer. Come now, let us kill him and throw him into one of the pits; then we shall say that a wild animal has devoured him, and we shall see what will become of his dreams'" (Genesis 37:17–20).

I love that the Bible spits truth about how dysfunctional and awful Joseph's family is rather than pretending (like we do much of the time) that it isn't. So many people's families—my own included—are hives of rejection, abuse, secrets, and wounds. Joseph's story sets us free to yell the truth from a mountaintop: FAMILY CAN SUCK. Accepting this suckiness and being up front about it is part of what it means to witness to radical *agape* in an airbrushed world. Yet this does not mean a loss of hope—far from it.

Every time we show love to others despite not having been shown that love ourselves, we turn into meteors. We burn off suckiness, leaving a trail of glow in our wake.

Joseph taught me this lesson. I believe God gives Joseph's story to comfort and guide those of us whose families of origin reject our personhood, gifts, dreams, and/or rainbow-colored coats. Joseph's brothers despised his dreams. When he took them to their door, they rejected not only them but him, and sold him for twenty bucks (okay, shekels, but you get the point). While most people give up on the dreams their families ridicule or hate, Joseph refused to abandon his as useless or unneeded by the world. Instead, even in Egypt, where he was a prisoner, he kept on doing what he did best and what he believed God called him to do. He remained a dreamer.

Eventually, the Egyptians—who were not Joseph's original family—recognized Joseph's offering for the amazing thing it was: a gift from God to be shared with others. No doubt, Joseph's own clan—the Israelites—had taught him that the Egyptians were their sworn enemies. They were not blood. Joseph didn't give a hoot; he made them his framily anyway. He married an Egyptian woman and started a new family of his own. "Joseph named the firstborn Manasseh, 'For,' he said, 'God has made me forget all my hardship and all my father's house.' The second he named Ephraim, 'For God has made me fruitful in the land of my misfortunes'" (Genesis 41:51–52).

In a dream, God told Joseph to save enough grain for a forthcoming famine, and Joseph listened. When the famine came, Joseph's dream-gift fed people and saved lives. Half-starved, Joseph's bio-family knocked at his door with their empty bowls. Joseph let them in and said, "I am your brother, Joseph, whom you sold into Egypt. And now do not be distressed, or angry with yourselves, because you sold me here; for God sent me before you to preserve life" (Genesis 45:4–5). In the end, Joseph's dream saved even those who once rejected it.

If Joseph were here today, he might leave us with this advice about framily and a love without limits.

1. Let yourself dream.
2. Don't let anyone shame you into taking off your coat of many colors. Rock your rainbow.
3. When you can no longer survive, leave home. Don't feel guilty if you need to love your family of origin from a distance. In God's eyes the entire world is your family.
4. Your life can always bear fruit, even in the land of your misfortunes.
5. Never forget: "When your mother and father forsake you, the Lord takes you up" (Psalm 27:10).
6. When your biological family hurts you, remember their hunger. When you're ready, open the door. In a world starved for love, forgiveness is food.
7. If the family you were born into can't right now value your gifts or dreams or personhood, God gives you permission to find a new clan who will. Let them adopt you.
8. Look at my life and remember: you can learn as much from love's famine as you can from its flourishing.

Chapter 4

WEARING THE WRONG NAMETAG (GRANDMA PERKINS)

*Do not fear, for I have redeemed you; I have
called you by name, you are mine.*

—Isaiah 43:1

What's in a name? When it comes to the radical love to which God calls us, pretty much everything. My grandmother taught me this lesson, though she never intended to.

My real name is Jacqueline, which is the feminine version of Jacob. But everybody called me Jackie growing up. For the first fifteen years of my life, I did too. At the time, I was a people-pleaser and believed that names were like presents—something you should let other people choose for you rather than pick for yourself. Even so, Jackie was a gift I desperately longed to return to the store or bury in the backyard. I wanted everyone to call me Jacqueline instead, but nobody would. I never understood why. Too many syllables? Nope. I had plenty of friends called Elizabeth and Jennifer, and even a friend named Jacqueline (whom I envied beyond all reason). I came to assume that because I was short (which I hated), I had to accept a short name (which I also hated).

As a teenager, I unhappily resigned myself to the fact that no one would ever call me by the name I wanted to be called. Still, I wasn't going down without a fight. If I had to go by a name I hated, I could at least spell it like I wanted, more like Jacqueline. And so, at age sixteen, I changed the spelling. Henceforth on all official teenage documents (letters to friends, hastily written Post-it notes to my mother, and pre-algebra homework) I was Jacquie. My friends went along with the change right away. My family, not so much. A year ago, a full three decades after the spelling change, my bio-father sent me a letter still addressed to Jackie Bussie. I stared at the envelope in my hand for a long time, as if the postman had brought me a stranger's mail.

But there's more to the story. My grandmother—my mother's mother—never called me by my name. I don't mean Grandma Perkins never called me Jacqueline, I mean she never even made it to Jackie or Jacquie. Instead, she chose to call me by a name no one else on God's green earth ever did: Aileen. My middle name. As a kid, every time she did this, it felt like I'd looked in the mirror and seen reflected back the face of the tooth fairy, who everyone knew was not real but made-up. My grandmother never called anyone else in my family, including my cousins or siblings, by their middle name or by a name other than the one they always went by. She never even nicknamed anyone; for some strange reason, I was the one exception.

I only saw my grandmother once a year, if that, but each time I was shocked anew by her reckless name treason. One August morning when I was nine years old, we arrived in rural Indiana, after our long drive from Georgia. We went straight to Grandma Perkins's house. I hadn't seen her for a year and was eager to show off several new lost teeth. I was also excited to see her gazillion plants, her huge white fluffball of a dog Bear, and her cages of green and yellow parakeets.

As we stood in Grandma Perkins's garage, Bear decided to greet me with that unfortunate but signature dog hello of humping my leg. My grandmother ignored this indignity but added her own. "Aileen, how are you?" she asked. Soooo awkward. I can't remember how I answered her, if I ever did. Sad as it is to confess, I was never really comfortable at my grandma's house, and that discomfort didn't only have to do with Bear's libido. Visiting grandma's house was the kind of thing that I loved in anticipation, until I was actually there and had to answer to a name that was not my own.

The next morning when I got up, my grandma had already left to go pick up the neighbor's kids (her entire life, she made a living babysitting other people's kids at her home). I took this chance to explore her cluttered kitchen. It was piled high with old newspapers and *Better Homes & Gardens*, and even had a drawer filled with twist ties from what appeared to be decades of loaves of Wonder Bread. (There's a name now for what my grandma probably had—compulsive hoarding disorder—but back then we just called it messy.) Behind her telephone, I spotted a stack of old Christmas cards that included several family photo-cards my mom had sent out in previous years. I took one down. Here it is.

Looking at the photo, I did a double take, then a triple. The baby in this picture is me. The handwriting on the card is—unmistakably—my mother's. My mother had never once called me Aileen to my face or on Christmas cards she sent to anyone else, yet here was undeniable evidence that whenever she wrote to her own mother, she called me Aileen.

I was furious. I turned to my mom who was peeling an onion over the kitchen sink. "Mom, what's up with this card?" I asked. I thrust the proof of guilt in her face. My freckles darkened. "And why does Grandma always call me Aileen?" It was the first time I'd ever asked. Before she could answer either question I proclaimed, in my sassiest time-to-knock-Charlie-Brown-down Lucy voice: "MY NAME IS NOT AILEEN!!"

Behind my anger trembled a fervent hope, that my grandmother hid a story behind the name Aileen—like it was her best friend's name growing up or the name of her long-lost sister. A good reason to love the name. But no. My mother's answer resembled the ending of those movies you hate precisely because they aren't a real ending at all, only a fade-out into bewilderment.

My grandma, whose name was Alice, wanted all of her grandchildren to have names that started with A. That was the actual answer my mother gave. Alliteration. Alice preferred alliteration to acknowledgment. Alice adored awkwardness and alienation in place of accuracy and attentiveness. This appalling answer failed to satisfy even my nine-year-old self. To make matters worse, my mother mumbled this answer without conviction, as if she barely believed it herself. As I recall, she never even looked up from her onion-peeling.

If my grandmother had a better reason for calling me by the wrong name my entire life other than a poetic yearning for alliteration, that mysterious reason died with her. And as for why my mother went along with it? Well, that secret's sealed tight as the mason jars of rosehip jam those two made together every summer.

Now that I'm older, I realize I should've sat my grandma down and said, "Grandma, why do you call everyone by their right name except me? Please don't call me Aileen. It hurts my feelings not to be known by you." I regret that I never did this. My grandma was dead by the time I was sixteen, and in that short amount of time, I never mustered up the adolescent courage for such an adult confrontation.

When you know a nickname comes from a place of love and special relationship, it can sing—like when our spouse calls us "sweetheart" or "darling." But when you're unsure of its motivation, it can wound. Sadly, my grandma's failure to call me by my name forever scarred my relationship with her. I never considered her a person I knew. More to the point, she never knew me. I never felt comfortable enough to open up. I never wrote her long letters, like I did my other grandmothers, about my second-grade teacher Ms. Bittle, whom I adored but who left our school when she got pregnant, or the cute boy Brad I fell in love with at Bible camp. In some ways, I'm ashamed to admit such a small thing led to such a big scar; in other ways, not so much.

To be honest with you, I'm still struggling to make sense of these strange misnaming moments of my childhood and what they've taught me about love. Here's what I've come up with so far.

Real Love Calls People by Their Right Names

Love and right-naming go together like a bee and blossoms. To live the life of love without limits to which God beckons, we need to call people by the right names. To call others by the name they want to be called is one of the ways we love them. Pseudonyms lead to pseudo-relationships, and this is true not just for our relationships with people but with everything.

In 1518, Martin Luther, the founder of my tradition of Lutheranism, wrote that those who follow Jesus "are called to call things by their right names." Or as his words are sometimes translated, "to call a thing what it actually is." In other words, names matter. A lot. Like a crazy lot. According to Luther, we constantly fail to call things what they actually are and people by their right names. Instead we name them based on what we want or perceive them to be based on our own projections, fears, and uncertainty. We want to be in charge of naming, because to name is to control. This is not love, it's a power grab. As we well know from everyday introductions, there's only one true way to discern a person's true name, and that is to ask. Only that person—and the God of love—knows the name that he or she should be called.

Luther's right: the world would look completely different if even a small percentage of the time we all actually called things and people by their right names. Think of the way bullies on the playground or internet call people despicable, demeaning, wrong names. Or the way the media and politicians call people who die in war "casualties"; people without certain government documents "illegal aliens"; and the hunger of children in poverty "food insecurity." Or how countless genocides began with one powerful group of people calling another group of people "vermin" (the Holocaust) or "cockroaches" (Rwanda), or even by renaming cold-blooded murder as "ethnic cleansing" (Croatia). As these examples demonstrate, names may seem trivial, but in actuality, they're life-and-death.

My good friend Ray, who is transgender, has taught me how important names can be. Ray, like all of my openly trans friends and students who have transitioned from one gender to another, no longer goes by his birth name. (Some of my other trans friends go so far as to refer to their birth name as their "dead name.") Ray's Facebook profile, email, and website proudly proclaim to the world what he describes as his *real name*, which was given to him by friends (framily!) who love him.

When I asked Ray why he changed his name, he explained: "It seemed vital to me that people call me by that new name. . . . It made me feel seen to change away from a name that I disliked, and that had been given me by my family of origin, toward a name that my family of choice had bestowed on me." Then he made me laugh super hard by telling me this joke, "If someone's name is Richard and he asks you to call him Dick, if you still insist on calling him Richard, then it's *you* he should call Dick."

Some love-without-limits Christian churches honor the life-giving nature of name changes within the trans community. The Church of England, for example, is considering instituting name-changing ceremonies—similar to baptisms—for trans persons who are transitioning from one gender to another.[1] Susan Musgrove, a Church of England Christian who attempted suicide when she realized she was "in the wrong body," said this about the name-change ceremony her church held for her: "I can't describe how important the blessing, and the acceptance it represents, is to me. I know that not everybody in the wider church will be happy about it, but it is an acceptance of me in all the guises that make me up. And that for me means everything."[2]

We can't ignore the truth any longer: right names save lives.

In our day, to call people and things by their right names is the new radicalism. It's how we call evil out as the thing that unnames us. It's how we show God's radical love to people. It's a way of saying: yes, you matter. I see you. I acknowledge our shared humanity.

The Christian theologian Frederick Buechner tells a stunning story about one Sunday morning when he went up for Communion at church. Buechner felt distracted and not fully present. He writes, "I could hear the priest moving along the rail from person to person as I knelt there waiting for my turn. The body of Christ, he said, the bread of heaven. The body of Christ, he said, the bread of heaven. When he got to me, he put in another word. The word was my name. 'The body of Christ, Freddy, the bread of heaven.'"[3] This unexpected hearing of his name startled Buechner awake. Suddenly the gift of the bread was personal. Jesus gave life to Freddy, to him, yes him in particular in all his Freddyness. Hearing our names said in love makes us feel as if we are in the right place, at the right time. We feel included. Present. Seen. Valued. As if we belong.

When Mary Magdalene went to the tomb early Easter morning, she saw a man she mistook for the cemetery groundskeeper. But the second the man said her name, she knew he was Jesus. "Jesus said to her, 'Woman, why are you weeping? Whom are you looking for?' Supposing him to be the gardener, she said to him, 'Sir, if you have carried him away, tell me where you have laid him, and I will take him away.' Jesus said to her, 'Mary!' She turned and said to him in Hebrew, 'Rabbouni!' (which means Teacher)" (John 20:15–16). To name is to know.

Names have immense power, as Jesus' own tradition of Judaism recognized. The Hebrew word for *name* (*shem*) appears a whopping 864 times in the Hebrew Bible. Rabbi Benjamin Blech explains, "Names represent our identity. . . . They define us. . . . They are to some extent prophetic. They capture our essence. They are the keys to our soul."[4] In the Jewish understanding, our true names come from God.

Jesus grasped the importance of names better than anyone. He often gave his closest companions special names, unique keys to their souls. For example, Jesus renamed Simon: "Jesus . . . looked at him and said, 'You are Simon son of John. You are to be called Cephas' (which is translated Peter)" (John 1:42). And Jesus also renamed John: "So he appointed the twelve: . . . John the brother of James (to whom he gave the name Boanerges, that is, Sons of Thunder)" (Mark 3:16–17). The disciples themselves cherished these new names because they discerned their deeper meaning: Jesus had gotten to know them well enough to give them nicknames—names that empowered and claimed them as his.

Jesus, in contrast, was surrounded by people who failed to call him by the right name. The Roman soldiers who murdered Jesus mocked him with the sarcastic name "king of the Jews." Even the disciples often screwed up his name:

> Now when Jesus . . . asked his disciples, "Who do people say that the Son of Man is?" And they said, "Some say John the Baptist, but others Elijah, and still others, Jeremiah or one of the prophets." He said to them, "But who do you say that I am?" Simon Peter answered, "You are the Messiah, the Son of the Living God." And Jesus answered him, "Blessed are you, Simon son of Jonah! For flesh and blood has not revealed this to you, but my Father in heaven." (Matthew 16:13–17)

Why was Jesus so obsessed with asking people, "Who do you say that I am?" Why did he care what other people called him? He wanted us to realize two things. One, the only right answer to what someone's real name is: the name God calls them. Simon Peter didn't give a hoot what other people called Jesus, he cared only about what God called Jesus, which was "son of God" and "Messiah." "For flesh and blood has not revealed this to you, but my father in heaven." Simon Peter is the one who gets this answer right, because he knows firsthand what it was like to be renamed by the God of love. The message is clear: we see people for who they really are only when we see them as God sees them. And though with all our might we resist putting on our God-glasses and calling other people by their right names, God's name for every single person on earth is "my beloved child."

And two, naming other people wields power, and power can be both liberating and dangerous. Does Jesus ask other people who they think he is because he wants other people to define him? Unlikely. Jesus knows darn well who he is. He asks, then, not because other people's answers will tell him who *he* is, but because their answers will tell him everything about who *they* are. Jesus is savvy. He understands that few things reveal more about you than the names you use to describe people different from yourself.

Think of all the wounding names people today call those who experience homelessness, those who live in poverty, women, people of color, immigrants, people with disabilities, people who are LGBTQ, people who are from other countries, people of a different religion, people of the opposing political party. Trailer trash. Bum. Welfare queen. Commie. Lunatic. Scum. Infidel. Idiot. R**ard. Fa**ot. Wetback. Wingnut. Whore. N-word. Pig. (And plenty more I'd never want to put in print.) These names belong to no one. No one wants these names, nor should we ever use them. Julia Dinsmore, who grew up in poverty, wrote a beautiful poem whose title says it all: "My Name Is Child of God, Not 'Those People.'"[5]

When Jesus hears us hurl these wrong names, Jesus becomes like that don't-mess-with-me mama who, child in front of her, faces down her child's bully and asks, "Come again? What did you call my child when no one else was around?" Jesus—let there be no doubt—is always around. He stands with arms locked tight around everyone we've called by these wrong names, and he asks us to answer to his face, *Who do you say that we are?* Every nasty name we've ever called someone on social media or in a fit of rage, Jesus considers a name we've called *him*: "Truly I tell you, just as you did it to one of the least of these . . . you did it to me" (Matthew 25:40).

You know that TV game show *Family Feud*? How when players give the wrong answer that buzzer obnoxiously blares *Benhhhh* and a massive red X flashes on the screen? Yep, that's God's reaction to our nasty name-calling. To our vain and sinful attempt to throw someone out of God's family and create an exception to God's no-exception love. God's buzzer must be getting worn out. The correct answer has never changed, but even after two thousand years, we still flunk the test. Who am I? Who is she? Who are they? Any answer other than "beloved child of God" is *always* the wrong answer.

To love is to listen. Often, what we misname political correctness is simply a person requesting that we call them by the name they (or God) have chosen for themselves. Many of my Native American friends, for example, decided a long time ago they didn't want to be called *Indians* (a misnomer if there ever was one). A friend of mine in a wheelchair doesn't want to be called *handicapped*, he prefers *person with a disability* or *wheelchair-user*. Many of my friends of African descent decided a long time ago that they preferred to be called *African Americans* rather than various insulting names of old, which I won't dignify by typing. Recently my white friend whose name is Sloane rolled her eyes at the name *African American*. "Why do they want to be called something different?" she objected. "We're all Americans, so why don't they just want to be called that?" I thought, *well, probably for the same reason we don't all want to be called "Sloane."*

To radically love folks as Jesus loves them is to let *them* decide what names they want to be called, and not to make that decision ourselves. Also, to not respond with an eye-roll when people change those names over time. Love is patient. Love is kind. We don't know who God is calling any of us to become. Respecting this has nothing to do with political correctness and everything to do with people. Or better, with loving them.

For people of faith, names are sacred. In the book *Getting to the Heart of Interfaith: The Eye-Opening, Hope-Filled Friendship of a Pastor, a Rabbi, and an Imam,* the imam contends that everyone possesses a sacred name—a true name that captures the gift of the Divine Breath within us.[6] He explains that when he was little, he often felt sad, small, and self-critical. His parents taught him to choose a term of endearment—such as *beloved*—for himself and then, in those hard moments, to address himself in his mind with this sacred name.[7] The purpose of calling ourselves by our sacred name—the name we believe God calls us by—is to restore our sense of the presence of God and to remind ourselves we are cherished.

When I teach *Getting to the Heart of Interfaith* in class, I give each of my students a blank nametag and ask them to write their sacred name on it. I encourage them to take the nametag home and look at their true name whenever they feel small, unloved, or alone. Last time we did this activity, I wrote down two for myself: "Daughter of Charlotte," and "Child of Grace."

Once when I was a little girl, my brother let the cat out of the bag that I was, as he put it, an accident. (I'm ten years younger than my sister and five years younger than him.) To me, an accident was a horrible thing—something that happened when knees got bloodied or cars crashed. Though I never would've admitted it, I wore this nametag *Accident* around for years, until the day I asked my mom about it. She hugged me and said, "Scientist Alexander Fleming discovered penicillin when it accidentally grew in his lab. Sometimes accidents are the best things that could ever happen to you."

What is the nametag you usually wear? Does it have written on it in black Sharpie *Unlovable* or *Not-Good-Enough* or *Failure* or *Stupid*? Here's what God wants you to do right now with all the wrong nametags that human miscarriages of love—either your own or someone's else—have forced you to wear: (1) Rip them off. (2) Insert them in the nearest paper shredder. (3) Replace them with the right one that only the divine can hand you. "And you shall be called by a new name that the mouth of the Lord will give" (Isaiah 62:2). Real love renames everything, even you.

What is your sacred name? When you figure out what it is, write it down on a nametag. Store it in a place where you can easily find it, and carry it with you in your pocket or purse on days when you need to be reminded. Next time your inner critic starts to beat you up for all the usual suspect reasons, take a breath and say *[insert sacred name here], you are loved*. You are, you know. Loved. Loved by a God who is Love itself. We must never forget our sacred names, or the fact that everybody has one. God names the whole world, no exceptions.

Real Love Understands Sometimes Names Gotta Change

Real love gets that sometimes we change and grow, and old names no longer fit. Unfortunately, the people around us often get scared when we start to evolve. They resist the change in our personhood by (symbolically) insisting on calling us by the old (wrong) names. Radical love, however, not only acknowledges growth but delights in it. Love even celebrates the change with a new name.

Human beings like to whine, "People never change," but God—alleluia!—believes in such a glorious possibility. In the scriptures, people often change, and God changes their names at the same time—as if to say, *hey skeptics, take note, it does happen!* Sometimes, God changes people's names while bestowing on their life a new purpose or calling. Other times, the people appear to have outgrown their old name. I like to believe that when folks in the scriptural stories get new names, they've so radically opened themselves up to a fresh start that even God has to call them something new.

Take, for example, the apostle Paul. He originally went by his Hebrew name, Saul. Saul spent his entire adult life persecuting Jesus' followers for heresy, until the day he was struck blind by a seizure he had in the street. Saul interpreted his misfortune as a sign from God that he was on the wrong path and "blind" to the truth that Jesus really was the long-awaited messiah (Acts 9:15–19). Through this experience, Saul became the most avid evangelist of Jesus' radical vision of love. He transformed in an instant from purest prosecutor to prolific promoter. From that point forward, he walked all over the Roman Empire spreading the message of radical love not only to the Jews but also to the gentiles, which was taking Jesus' message further than anyone before him had ever done. Saul's reversal was not just a 180, but a triple axel.

To spotlight Saul's gold-medal turn around, Saul begins going by his Roman (Latin) name, Paul, instead of his Hebrew name, Saul. No one knows whether Paul "changed" it or God did, but one thing's clear: they're both cool with the shift. Paul understands better than anyone he's not the same person anymore: "The one who formerly was persecuting us is now proclaiming the faith he once tried to destroy" (Galatians 1:23). Paul's rejection of his former self is so complete my mind imagines him traveling the streets of Rome and running into an old pal. "Saul!" the old friend cries out. "Please don't call me that," begs Paul-formerly-known-as-Saul, sick at the memory of himself that the old name conjures up. "I am Paul now," he corrects, lifting his chin. "Let me tell you why."

One of my friends since childhood recently emerged from a heartbreaking marriage. Once her divorce was finalized, she started introducing herself to new people as Pamela instead of Madison, her given name. I recall my shock the first time I overheard a new friend greet her, "Hey Pam!" At first, this felt weird and I almost begrudged her this re-creation of herself. But then, I remembered how, without skipping a beat, she had changed the spelling of my name from Jackie to Jacquie on all the letters she wrote to me back in high school, simply because I had asked her to.

I recently asked Pamela about her name change, and it was one of the best talks we've ever had. Pamela explained that she didn't like the angry, resentful person she'd become at times in her previous marriage. She said that she liked the name Pamela because it meant *loving* and *kind*. For her, a new name signified a new start. "Since we believe that Christ died for all, we also believe that we have all died to our old life. . . . This means that anyone who belongs to Christ has become a new person. The old life is gone; a new life has begun!" (2 Corinthians 5:14–17 NLT).

This name-change story reminds me that God—unlike the rest of us—never says, *Hey, stop growing, you're scaring me!* Instead, God celebrates our metamorphosis (or, as our trans friends might call it, our transition) with sparklers and a banner bearing our new name in all caps.

It happens in life, thank God, that we outgrow certain selves. Hope means we can shed former selves like old skin. Love lets us release the outworn.

When I was a kid growing up in Georgia, we liked to play pranks with the cicadas' shed skin-casings we found in the woods. The little body clung to a tree with its sharp claws and made you believe it was a real bug, until you picked it up and realized that your hand held nothing but an empty shell. *Exoskeletons*, explained our science teacher. The insect had to leave its exoskeleton behind, because it was too hard and rigid to allow for growth or change. For us humans, former names—especially the names we were once called by someone who hurt, abused, neglected, or misunderstood us—are exoskeletons. We must cast them off, for no one lives inside any longer.

Sometimes in the biblical stories, God calls people by a new name even *before* the metamorphosis, which is the strongest vote of confidence you could ever cast in a person's potential. It's like naming your diary *"New York Times* Best Seller" or naming your newborn "Secretary of State" or "Olympic Gold Medalist." It's preposterous and presumptuous, but lucky for us that's how God works. God's love sees us for who we can become, instead of merely the person we are today, unfinished.

Take, for example, Sarai and Abram, the mother and father of the Jewish and Christian faiths. In Genesis, they're called Sarai and Abram until God changes both of their names when they're called to leave everything behind and head for the promised land. Sarai is over a hundred years old and barren when God shows up at the couple's tranquil tent and promises them descendants as innumerable as the stars. Although Sarai isn't even pregnant yet, God renames Sarai (a name some scholars say means *contentious,* or *barren*) Sarah, meaning *princess.* God says to Abraham, "As for Sarai your wife, you shall not call her Sarai, but Sarah shall be her name. I will bless her, and moreover I will give you a son by her. . . . She shall give rise to nations; kings of peoples shall come from her" (Genesis 17:15–16).

Similarly, Abram (meaning *ancestor,* or *father*) becomes Abraham (meaning *ancestor of a multitude*) at the moment God establishes a covenant with him and the Hebrew people. "No longer shall your name be Abram, but your name shall be Abraham; for I have made you the ancestor of a multitude of nations" (Genesis 17:5). Like many women (and increasingly, men) who change their name to signal a new marriage relationship with their spouse, God changes Sarai's and Abram's names to reflect that they have been chosen to be in a new covenant relationship with the Divine. Like today's Facebook status update *In a relationship,* a scriptural name change signified the same, but with God.

While we're calling things by their right names, let's note that the Bible calls Abraham "the Hebrew" and considers him the father of the Hebrew people (Genesis 14:13). The word Hebrew— *ivrit*—comes from a root meaning *to cross over a boundary;* the word thus means *resident in a foreign land.* In other words, *Hebrew means immigrant.* Abraham and Sarah are the first immigrants, the first "resident aliens." For Christians and Jews who claim these two as faith-parents, this means our faith is an immigrant faith! It also means we were born to cross boundaries.

The second person in the Bible to be referred to as a Hebrew— as an immigrant—is Joseph, who, as we know, ends up living in Egypt, a country not his homeland. If, as the Bible claims, God's chosen people are the Jews—the Hebrews—then the people God calls "a light to the nations" (Isaiah 49:6) are none other than *immigrants.* God goes out of God's way to rename as *beloved* the people others have named *other* and *alien* and *foreigner*. The people who have had to leave their homeland and live in a far country not of their birth. "The foreigner residing among you must be treated as your native-born. Love them as yourself, for you were foreigners in Egypt. I am the Lord your God" (Leviticus 19:34 NIV).

Uh-oh. Do our hearts and national and global policies today toward refugees and immigrants reflect this commandment? Calling people by their right names radically enlarges the scope of our love—and our sphere of responsibility. Which is precisely, I would guess, why we broken people avoid doing it. Recently, I saw the most powerful sign welcoming refugees hung out in front of a Lutheran church in Fargo, North Dakota. Here it is:

When I think back on my own name and the way it's changed over the years, my story has a two-part joy ending. First, nowadays almost everyone calls me Jacqueline (more on that in a later chapter). Though during my younger years nearly everyone in my life refused to call me Jacqueline, there were always a few loving outliers.

When I was a teenager, my best friend (now husband) Matt always addressed me as Jacqueline on cards or letters. My mother, surprisingly, hardly ever called me by the full name she herself gave me. But while I was in college, she once tucked into one of her letters a cut-out newspaper article about the best names to give your child if you wanted them to flourish. The number one recommended name for girls was Jacqueline. My mother circled the name Jacqueline in red. Never prone to flattery, my mother wrote this sentence in the accompanying letter (which I have saved to this day): "You are so talented." It's no coincidence that the two people who made me feel most cherished in this life are the same two who taught me to treasure my real name.

Second, my grandmother. I find letter writing, even to those who are no longer living, healing and edifying. So, while writing this chapter, I decided to write my grandma a letter. The experience forever changed my attitude toward her and the name Aileen.

In the letter, I told my grandma that she had hurt me, and then I asked her why she called me Aileen. On the spur of the moment, I decided to answer this question by writing with my left hand. In a writing workshop I took a few years ago from my dear friend, spiritual director, and adopted mom Helen Beth, she taught me the compassion-generating technique of writing with your nondominant hand when you want to hear the voice of someone else. The idea is that by giving up your dominant hand, you stop dominating the conversation with your own point of view.

By the end of my left-hand writing, I was sobbing my eyes out. I hadn't cried about my grandma since the day she died thirty-one years ago. I know it sounds crazy. But sometimes you have to get out of your own way, you know? Here's what it looked like on the page.

And here's an excerpt, unedited (except for length).

RIGHT HAND: *Grandma, why did you call me Aileen?*

LEFT HAND: *Because I never got to name anything.*

RIGHT: *But that's not true, is it? Didn't you name your kids? Your pets?*

LEFT: *I did but other people named over me. Richard was named G.I., Joyce was named injured, and Charlotte well I put all my hopes in her she was so smart but I wanted her to be named college graduate and death stole that from all of us and I asked her to return home so she did. I felt so guilty when that meant she never returned and the dream died, along with a little bit of us. . . . Later her life took her so far away I lost everything Alfred to the grave Richard to war Charlotte to him Joyce to sorrow. I tried to surround myself with little things—things that needed me—my dog Bear and Polly the parakeet and the neighbor boy in the pac-n-play I kept everything I could and I lined my house the walls of my heart with them like a fortress because Indiana winters were so long and so gray and I didn't want to burden anyone and can't you see I tried? I wished even the twist ties might come in handy and tie me back together or tie me to the love I almost had or the hopes me and Alfred had for our kids. Charlotte was the apple of our eye and when she got lost I got lost too and it felt like the fight left me so I loved the plants and the birds and I loved them hard I took the gray hair off my own head and wrapped it around their little green stems because I read it could feed them and I talked to the plants—remember how I taught you that? My oxygen helped them grow. This is what you do when the world takes all, you love small. And now you—your name that too was loving small just letters in a mouth a mouth that was so empty I never meant no harm I just wanted to name something for once I just wanted to love something like it was mine to name and you were small like the birds so I thought I could get away with it. . . . It feels* *sad to never have a say. Who is a woman to say if her son has to go to war or her husband has to leave please know I all I wanted was to finally have a say Jackie it's all I ever wanted.*

Something happened to me while I wrote these words. A Holy Spirit takeover. The hard shell of my heart cracked. Compassion pierced the tight skin of my anger and got born in the world with a wail.

The left-hand writing made me feel as if I was looking through God's peephole into my grandma's heart. I can't say if anything I saw there was true. I can only say that for the first time, I cared enough to stretch up on my tippy-toes and peer in.

After I stopped crying-writing, I called my beloved adopted mom Helen Beth to thank her for teaching me left-hand writing and to share what had happened. Helen Beth was very moved. The next day she called me back and asked me how much I knew about the name Aileen. "Nothing," I answered, "except that it means *light*." Helen Beth said, "Well, it's Irish." I was shocked. I didn't know that. My grandmother was Irish. She cherished her Irish heritage. I remembered attending her big Irish family reunion once as a kid. Helen Beth continued. "The name has two meanings," she said: *Bringer of Light* and *She knows*. Hearing this, I got chills.

As if that weren't enough, after I hung up the phone with Helen Beth, I did a little research of my own. I discovered that Aileen is the Irish version of *Helen*. Until that moment, I'd never realized I share a name with my surrogate mom, who's one of the people I love most in this world.

My grandma was right: I do know, at last. Real love renames everything, even your past.

Chapter 5

ADOPTION (ELIJAH)

Let us consider how we may spur one another on toward love and good deeds . . . encouraging one another.
—Hebrews 10:24–25

He destined us for adoption as his children through Jesus Christ, according to the good pleasure of his will, to the praise of his glorious grace.
—Ephesians 1:5–6

As I sit at my front window sipping my tea, I see my neighbors, Jim and Jennifer, out for a walk. They've been together twenty years, since they were teenagers. They're devout Presbyterians. Every Sunday, they walk down the road to a little white church with a bright green door. Their little son Elijah, with the carrot-colored hair, toddles between them, dapper in his miniature blue suit and tie. Watching them makes me smile. The love bouncing off their family challenges the sun to a duel of light.

Elijah's parents don't share his ginger hair because Elijah is adopted.

Jim and Jennifer's adoption process was a prolonged, emotional roller-coaster ride that often left them frazzled. Their two-year journey to find Elijah taught me a lot that I didn't know. For instance, the adoption process can feel like one of those terrifying online dating apps—swipe right for yes, swipe left for no. "But it's really true!" Jim and Jennifer told me one day, only half-laughing at the comparison. With their particular agency, adoption was a match process. Translation: the birth parent or parents have to choose the couple they want to adopt their baby from a long list of available couples, and likewise, the adoptive couple has to say yes to that particular baby.

Jim and Jennifer told me all about the day they first signed up with the adoption agency. Much like Match.com, the agency interviewed them to complete their profile regarding what babies they were willing to take. "What race baby do you have in mind?" the social worker asked them, pen in hand.

"Any," my friends replied, holding each other's hands.

"Good!" she exclaimed with a smile. "That will shorten your wait. Boy or girl?"

"Either!" they blurted out in unison.

"Health problems? Disabilities?" she asked, peering over the rim of her reading glasses to ensure they were taking the question seriously.

"Yes," they said simply. "Yes."

As you can tell, my neighbors have outsize hearts. All those huge hearts wanted was a tiny, breathing baby to swaddle.

Over the many long months, Jim and Jennifer were disappointed lots of times. Birth parents kept saying no to them. Every time they didn't match, they felt rejected. But they didn't let that stop them. They kept putting themselves out there again and again—until finally there was a match, with Elijah.

Elijah's life had a hard beginning. His birth mother suffered from numerous addictions, including drugs and alcohol. At the time Elijah was born, she was in prison for numerous felonies. Elijah was her third child, none of whom were in her custody. Very late in her pregnancy with Elijah, she regularly smoked crack and drank. This meant that when Elijah was born, he suffered from fetal alcohol syndrome and cocaine withdrawal. Elijah was born premature, in prison. From the moment his lungs sucked air, Elijah's birth mother placed him in an adoption plan. Once Elijah was released from the prison hospital, he went into foster care, where he awaited a family to adopt and love him as their own.

When Elijah was placed into the adoption process, the folks at the agency worried. Experienced in their job of matchmaking, they were all too aware of the common prejudice against babies with fetal alcohol syndrome and the stigma of the ugly slur "crack baby." Through absolutely no fault of their own, children with fetal alcohol syndrome can develop a whole host of problems—development delays, irritability, low birth weight, learning disabilities, sleep disorders, attention deficit disorders, possible drug and alcohol addiction.

The social workers at the agency knew that not all babies develop these problems, but that even the possibility of them was more than many young couples are willing to take on. In the adoption world, such at-risk children are often categorized as "hard to place." Many hard-to-place babies do not match with anyone for months, sometimes years, sometimes forever. The agency was worried the same might happen to little Elijah.

And it did, at first. Many, many couples who were on the list ahead of Jim and Jennifer said no to little Elijah. But then the agency called Jim and Jennifer, and they said yes. When they brought him home and let me hold him for the first time, the theologian Karl Barth's one-sentence summary of the gospel popped into my head: "The first and last word is Yes and not No."[1]

The first year was not pretty. Elijah was a handful. He was often sick and irritable. He experienced delays in learning to talk and walk. Whenever Jim and Jennifer came over, I worried about them. The permanent dark circles under their eyes were the ominous purple of bruises. Looking at them reminded me of that line from Dostoevsky, "Love in action is a harsh and dreadful thing compared to love in dreams."

But more than anything, I stood in awe of my two dear friends. They loved little Elijah fiercely, through every sleepless night. They never stopped praying. They never stopped asking Matt and me to pray for their son, or for them, or for Elijah's mom, whom they often visited in prison (whether she wanted them to or not). They never lost faith in their conviction that God had called them to be Elijah's parents.

One night, Jim told me that he believed coincidences are not coincidences at all, but God winking at the world. In the mouth of anyone else, I would have been put off by this cliché, but instead I took it to heart. I somehow knew that Jim had earned the right to say it. Deep down, I also knew that Jim and Jennifer had done something I would have been too afraid to do. It shames me to even have to look at this confession of mine on the page. My neighbors' brave act of capacious *agape*-love brought them a joy so luminous, I could see it as they walked down the sidewalk to church.

Now. If I asked you what adjectives you would use to describe Jim and Jennifer, what would you say? Awesome? Faithful? Inspiring? Phenomenal? Would you say that Jim and Jennifer are an amazing Christian couple? An incredible example of Jesus' love laboring and stretching the world past its usual limits?

I certainly would. In fact, I would go so far as to wager that God up and plunked Elijah's parents right smack in the middle of our neighborhood in order to show us that radical love is not a fairy tale but a family. But here's the truth. Some of my neighbors would not have used any of the nice terms I just used to describe Elijah's parents. In fact, they would say—and often did—that they were downright offended by the sight of Elijah and his parents walking down the street on Sunday mornings.

What? I hope you're thinking. *You've got to be kidding.*

No, I'm not. The reason that some folks felt that way is because although I've told you the truth in the story of Elijah's parents, I've changed one small detail: their names aren't Jim and Jennifer. Those are fake names I made up. *Who cares!* you're probably thinking. *Simply changing their names doesn't change a thing about the story!*

I certainly believe that's true. But let me tell you their real names so you can decide for yourself. Elijah's parents' real names are Brian and Bob. Elijah's adoptive parents are two men.

Does this change the way you feel about Elijah's adoption? Or about his parents? It probably doesn't for you, but the sad part is, for some folks, that fact changes everything. So much so that they censor it. Yep, this book's original publisher was so scandalized by this true story of Elijah's adoption that they demanded I cut it. Not a part of it. I mean all of it. Every. Single. Word. Rather than submit this story to their scalpel, I put this entire book up for adoption . . . to a new publisher. (And fortunately, found it a new home.)

According to data from the National Register—the national database of children available for adoption and approved adopters waiting for children—LGBTQ people are more willing to consider adopting hard-to-place children than straight people.[2] Brian and Bob told me that the folks at their adoption agency claimed this was the case, explaining that they routinely place hard-to-place children in homes with gay parents, simply because no one else will take them. Those gay couples usually weren't even the birth parent's first choice; most of the time the straight birth parents only went down that road as a last resort.

Many speculate that this exceptional willingness on the part of LGBTQ couples to adopt hard-to-place kids is that they draw water from a compassionate well of understanding—an understanding of what it feels like to be unwanted, to not belong. When I asked Brian about it, he said, "Gay people know all about what it's like to feel unloved. Of course gay couples are willing to adopt the kids the straight couples don't want. Most of our parents are straight, and many of them don't want us."

No one can understand the rejected as well as the rejected. This is why Jesus was willing to become one of the rejected, so there'd be no sad corner within us where his love wouldn't fit. In Jesus, all hard-to-place people find a home. "In my Father's house there are many dwelling places. If it were not so, would I have told you that I go to prepare a place for you? And if I go and prepare a place for you, I will come again and will take you to myself, so that where I am, there you may be also" (John 14:2–3).

In our country today, nearly half a million children are in foster care. According to a recent UCLA study, an estimated two million gay and lesbian couples in America would like to adopt children. Many birth parents who have a say in the matter still choose not to place their children with same-sex couples. In some states, until 2016(!), it was illegal for same-sex couples to adopt. In 2015, it was declared unconstitutional to deny gay couples the right to marry (and thus adopt), but even now that ruling is being challenged in the courts. And there are many people— predominantly evangelical Christians—who would like to see it overturned. All I can think of when I read these faceless dates and statistics is Elijah, who would still be in foster care if such Christians had had their way.

Author-activist Shane Claiborne once gave a moving speech on my college's campus. With tears in his eyes, he shared the results of a recent poll. When Americans were asked cold turkey to say what words pop into their head when they hear the word *Christian*, the top three answers were: (1) judgmental, (2) hypocritical, and (3) antigay. This is what it has come down to, my friends. This is what we are known for in this day and age. As far as I know, not a single person in the poll answered "adopting babies no one else wants" or "loving without limits."

Some Christians, when they talk about LGBTQ folks, never mention people like Brian and Bob, who not only love Jesus but also walk down the street holding the little hand of that love in a way that puts many of us straight people to shame.

I once heard it said, every double standard arises from one thing and one thing only—a deficiency of loving. Best. Definition. Ever.

When I was in tenth grade, my childhood friend Jess McCorkin and I were sitting in her sister's car right outside ChiChi's, our favorite Mexican restaurant and high-school hangout. Out of nowhere, Jess asked me, "What do you think about homosexuality?" I had been raised in a home, school, and community of folks who believed homosexuality was a sin. Therefore, in an effort to be a good A+ Christian, I regurgitated the only answer I had ever been taught, "Well, the Bible says it's wrong," I said. Jess didn't look at me. She looked straight ahead out the windshield, as if forcing her face to go as expressionless as a tortilla. "Let's go inside," she said, and jumped out of the car. Jess and I never spoke again about sexuality. Years later, I realized that I hadn't actually answered her question.

I am haunted by this incident. I have failed a lot of friends in my life, but sometimes I fear I failed Jessica most of all. Although it was not clear to me at the time, it seems likely to me now that Jess was gay. Jess has never attended a single one of our high-school reunions. I have no idea where she is, and none of my high-school friends do either. I have tried to find her, because I want to apologize—for so many things, for not even having asked her why she asked me that question. But perhaps most of all, for not having told her I loved her, no matter what.

I think of Jess a lot because of the work I do every day. I teach theology and ethics to college students. Those years from eighteen to twenty-two are an important time when a lot of young people are in the process of finding themselves, of discovering—and owning—their sexual identities. I am fortunate; a lot of my students trust me enough to confide in me about their deepest struggles.

We believe words are raindrops—things that softly roll down our arm and, given time, evaporate. But this is a lie. Words are buckshot, able to embed themselves forever into our flesh. My students have taught me this better than anyone.

Jeremy

Let me introduce you to Jeremy. In my third year of teaching, Jeremy was the finest student in my Christian Ethics class. In addition to being smart, he was star of the football team, kind to everyone, and therefore, immensely popular. He was a devout Christian who came from a churchgoing, God-loving home. He was the homecoming king, and all the girls swooned over him. One day in my course, we were discussing gay marriage. As I always did with every hot topic, I assigned essays written by diverse Christians who held opposing views on the subject.

After class, Jeremy came to my office. "Say what? Christians who are LGBTQ-affirming? Before today, I never knew such people existed," he said. We talked for the next two hours.

A few weeks later, Jeremy came out to me as a gay man. I was the first person he ever told, and I consider it a gift and honor that he confided in me. Sitting across from me in my office with my box of Kleenex in his lap, Jeremy vividly described for me what his life was like growing up. He never let himself date boys. Instead, he dated girls. He not only tried to feel attracted to them, he prayed for it. Most nights, he would lie in bed, sobbing and praying that God would make him straight. He went to a Christian therapist, who also tried to help to pray him straight. Nothing worked.

After years of praying but seeing no change, he worried that God had walked out on him, disgusted, the same way his parents said they would be if he ever dared bring a boy home with him. A life without God was a meaningless void for Jeremy. He decided that he wanted to die. He came up with a plan. He prayed that his attempt to make it happen would succeed. But this prayer too went unanswered—thank God.

Because of how much I cared about Jeremy, I did some homework. I learned that an estimated one-third of people who identify as LGBTQ have tried to commit suicide. I might never have learned this—or I might have learned it too late—had it not been for Jeremy. I referred to Jeremy earlier as my student, but that's not accurate. He was my teacher.

For some reason, this image of Jeremy lying in bed every night, with his prayer to be made straight going unanswered, grated my heart into shreds. Though I'm straight, I could connect to feeling haunted by secrets, and to the fear of living inside the jail of other people's judgment. Jeremy sincerely wanted to be a Christian who followed Jesus, but many people around him told him that because of who he was, he could not.

Let's get one thing straight: if our sins make us people who aren't "real Christians," then no one in this world is a Christian. "For all have sinned and fall short of the glory of God" (Romans 3:23).

Contrary to popular belief, the word *homosexuality* is not in the Bible. The Bible doesn't actually have a word for an enduring sexual orientation toward the same sex. Instead, the Bible speaks exclusively of same-sex sex acts, and only in six passages (Genesis 19:4–9; Leviticus 18:22, 20:13; Romans 1:24–27; 1 Corinthians 6:9–10; and 1 Timothy 1:9–10). The biblical writers appear to assume that everyone is naturally attracted to people of the opposite sex. They appear to have no concept that anyone could be gay or lesbian in our modern sense of the term.

For instance, in Romans, Paul condemns same-sex acts on the grounds that such acts are unnatural. "For this reason God gave them up to degrading passions. Their women exchanged natural intercourse for unnatural, and in the same way also the men, giving up natural intercourse with women, were consumed with passion for one another. Men committed shameless acts with men and received in their own persons the due penalty for their error" (Romans 1:26–27).

Many Christians and biblical scholars believe this passage should be interpreted in light of modern scientific insights, in the same way that even though the Bible suggests that mental illness is caused by demon possession, most contemporary Christians reject such a point of view. They note that modern science contends—based on genetic and biological research—that to be gay or lesbian is natural and not a choice.[3] Same-sex behavior does, after all, occur in many species of God's good creation, not just human beings.[4] If you believe the science that asserts that same-sex behavior is natural, then that changes how you read Paul's words. Seen in this light, Paul, who presumes that all people are straight, is arguing in the Romans passage that for straight people to engage in same-sex acts is unnatural. Using this same logic, it is likewise unnatural for gay people to engage in heterosexual acts.

Of course, plenty of Christians reject science and believe it has no place in biblical interpretation. I'm not one of them. But for their sake, let's sidestep science and take a closer look only at the verses that frame Paul's words in Romans 1, which are crucial but usually ignored.

In Romans 1:18, Paul writes, "For the wrath of God is revealed from heaven against all ungodliness and wickedness of those who by their wickedness suppress the truth." The operative word in this verse is *all*—*all* acts of ungodliness and wickedness incur the wrath of God. In verse 26, Paul mentions same-sex behaviors as one example of this ungodliness. In verse 29, he goes on to list others:

"They were filled with every kind of wickedness, evil, covetousness, malice. Full of envy, murder, strife, deceit, craftiness, they are gossips, slanderers, God-haters, insolent, haughty, boastful, inventors of evil, rebellious toward parents, foolish, faithless, heartless, ruthless. They know God's decree, that those who practice such things deserve to die—yet they not only do them but even applaud others who practice them" (Romans 1:29–32). Paul wraps the whole section up with this whopper, "Therefore you have no excuse, whoever you are, when you judge others; for in passing judgment on another you condemn yourself, because you, the judge, are doing the very same things" (Romans 2:1).

Paul's list of wicked behaviors is exhaustive. Before it, we all stand convicted. That is Paul's entire point in Romans. In the letter, he tries to convince his Jewish Christian friends that God has called him to bring the good news of salvation also to the gentiles. But Paul's Jewish Christian friends aren't having any of it; they believe that gentiles are beyond redemption because of their sinful ways. The gentiles, in other words, are an exception to redemption. Paul argues back that his Jewish friends are sinners too, just like the gentiles they condemn. No one, according to Romans, is beyond the reach of the gospel.

How ironic, then, that Christians have for centuries used Romans 1 to condemn only LGBTQ people to hell and never envious people, braggarts, gossips, or rebellious teens. Maybe it's because gay people are an easy target, a cheap shot. Most Christians are straight, but all Christians envy, brag, gossip, and rebel. Of all the things that Christians do that make me cry the hardest, this ranking of sins is one of them. Even if some straight people do think of gay people's sexual orientation as a sin, why do they see it as any worse than the sins straight people commit—very few of which get them thrown out of church?

When straight people focus only on the verse in Romans 1 that doesn't condemn them, they construct a moat around their personal fortress of righteousness and close the drawbridge. They forget that yes, the apostle Paul hated same-sex acts, but he hated hypocrisy just as much: "Why do you pass judgment on your brother? Or you, why do you despise your brother? For we will all stand before the judgment seat of God . . . each of us will give an account of himself to God. Therefore let us not pass judgment on one another any longer, but rather decide never to put a stumbling block or hindrance in the way of a brother" (Romans 14:10–13).

Jesus, unlike Paul, never utters a word about same-sex attraction or acts, let alone about sexual orientation. Jesus does, however, condemn divorce, or at least, remarriage. When the disciples ask if it's okay for a man to divorce his wife, Jesus answers, "Whoever divorces his wife and marries another commits adultery against her; and if she divorces her husband and marries another, she commits adultery" (Mark 10:11).

Today in America, which is predominantly Christian, half of all straight marriages end in divorce. Almost everyone in my family self-identifies as an evangelical Christian who believes the Bible is the word of God. And yet, going all the way back to my great-grandmother and all the way down to my siblings, nearly everyone in my family has been divorced and remarried, or has married a partner who has been divorced multiple times. Yet my family members do not judge each other for this (rightly, in my view). Nor have I ever heard one of them claim that divorce and remarriage are sinful. Here again, though: double standards = deficiency of loving.

Of course, the reason so many contemporary churches and believers accept divorce and remarriage is because they read Jesus' words in context. In first-century Palestine, men held all the power. They could divorce their wives for any reason, leaving them penniless and homeless with no legal recourse. Jesus doesn't care that this is legal, he deems it despicable. In Mark, Jesus speaks directly to men. When Jesus tells them it's not okay to divorce their wives, he summons them to a much higher standard of love and justice than even the law demands. Jesus' words don't *judge* women, they *protect* women. No doubt his words shocked his audience. By condemning divorce, Jesus stands up for the most vulnerable among us (in his day, women). Here as in everywhere in the Gospels, Jesus calls for a love that is both scandalous and radical.

Other Christians, many of them members of my own family, castigate me for holding what they consider terrible and sinful views on LGBTQ issues. These well-meaning folks worry about the state of my soul. They accuse me of cherry-picking biblical verses to support my point of view. They are right. I don't deny it. I don't take all of the Bible literally, nor do I follow all of its 600+ commandments. I am a self-confessed selective literalist. There's no pride in this statement, just honesty.

Almost daily I violate the biblical command not to wear cotton/polyester blends (Deuteronomy 22:11). When I eat bacon, I break the rule in Leviticus 11:8, which prohibits the eating of pork. Whenever I don my pearl necklace, braid my hair, or wear gold earrings, I flagrantly flout 1 Timothy 2:9. The apostle Paul says in the New Testament that women should not speak in church; however, prioritizing other passages in scripture, my Christian denomination (Lutheranism) ordains women. I myself have preached countless times.

All Christians cherry-pick the Bible. The real question is not who cherry-picks; it's who is honest enough to confess it? Who among us stones kids to death when they curse their parents, as Exodus 21:17 commands? If you're crying foul saying, *But that's the Old Testament! Jesus came along and changed all that!*, then try this one: How many of us do as Christ instructed in Mark 10:21 and sell all that we have and give it to the poor? He said *all* that we have, people. ALL.

Once we finally admit we're selective literalists, we can openly discuss what criteria we're using to justify our choices, and only then can we hold one another accountable to them. For me, I use the scriptural principle of *agape*, which Jesus says in Mark 12:31 is the most important of all: "'Love your neighbor as yourself.' There is no commandment greater." I measure all of scripture's other teachings, and all of my life, against this principle. I hold no illusion that I do this perfectly, but I try my best.

At a writing retreat a few years ago, the leader asked us to write for five minutes on the following prompt: *What's something you used to believe whole-heartedly, but now disbelieve just as whole-heartedly?* I wrote the following:

> I used to believe that if you were gay, you were a sinner and would go to hell. I believed this because I thought the Bible said so, completely ignoring that the Bible also says women who've been raped in cities should be stoned to death (Deuteronomy 22:23–24), as should kids who curse their parents (Leviticus 20:9). Believing this was like believing people with brown eyes or red hair were hell-bound sinners. It made God out to be a nasty bandit who willfully stole from people all that could save them. God the great Absconder of Salvation, God the Thief, God the Bully, God the Judge who hurts people by making them born a certain way but then denies all accountability, condemning them to prison forever for his own actions. The Bible says we're made in God's image; but back when I believed these things, *I* was the one who made God in mine.

Recently, in my religious autobiographies class, I asked each of my students to each write a six-word memoir on a card. Of the nearly quarter of a million words in the English language, here's the six that my student Sara Funkhouser chose to describe her life story:

Not long after we did this class activity, Sara confided to me that although a lot of Christians don't support LGBTQ ordination, she would like to become a pastor someday. Honestly, I could never live with myself if anything I ever said or did kept a person as spectacular as Sara out of the pulpit, let alone the pews.

A lot of people whom I love believe I'm wrong on all this. But I'm sticking with a radical love without limits anyway. That's my mantra for following Jesus in this messy yet marvelous world: above all else, *agape*.

Chapter Postscript

When I first started graduate school, I told my mentor that I would never be able to work for him or teach during the summers because I needed to spend the summers caring for my sick mother. He responded, "Well, it's about time someone stopped *talking* about love and *did* something about it." While writing this chapter, I decided to stop talking about my love for Jess McCorkin and do something about it. I determined to find her and apologize for what I had said—and not said—over thirty years go.

A Google search returned no hits. Jess was nowhere online. Then, thinking about my own adult name change, I wondered if she perhaps had changed the name she went by. I did a search only for her last name and jackpot: numerous hits. Apologizing silently for having become an internet stalker, I clicked on each link. One of the last sites I looked at was a tech company in Oregon, which had a picture of their employees. I zoomed in. There, unmistakably, was Jess McCorkin, standing shoulder to shoulder with her colleagues. I cried instantly at the sight of her face. She looked so—well, so marvelously happy.

Before I could talk myself out of it, I sent Jess a short email at her work. I reminded her who I was, and asked if she'd like to be in touch. I gave her my contact info and waited.

After a few weeks, she replied. She said of course she remembered me and gave me her personal email and phone.

Immediately, before I could chicken out, I sat down and composed my apology letter to Jess. I didn't make any assumptions about her sexuality, but I did say some things I say in this chapter. How sorry I was for what I had said that day, and for not having said I loved her, no matter what. How often I thought of her, and how I'd failed her. At the end, I asked how she was, and how her family, life, and job were.

Months passed. Jess didn't write me back. I fretted and panicked. I reread my email a hundred times, wondering where I had misstepped. Then one night amid my angst, I had a dream. I was standing next to Jess. I put my left arm around her and introduced her to some old high-school friends. *Here she is, y'all!!* I exclaimed. *And they've been together for eleven years!* I said, gesturing at a beautiful woman, standing off to the side. Jess smiled at the woman, and then at me. A smile so real that it woke me up with a start. I can't explain why, but when I awoke, a peace inside me whispered: *even if you never hear from Jess again, it's okay. The burden was always on you to apologize, never on her to respond.*

Another month passed. I finished this book. And then, when I least expected it, Jess's name appeared in my inbox. My heart leapt. This time the email was long. Jess said she didn't remember what I had said to her outside the Mexican restaurant that day, but that it was water under the bridge. She shared some tragic truths about her family, including that her parents and three older siblings had all died. She wrote that living without family was hard, but that she hoped maybe she and I could be adopted family to each other.

And then, Jess came out to me. She told me that six years ago she and her partner Patricia got married—and that they'd been together for *eleven wonderful years.*

A genuine apology is like an eleventh-hour rain on a dusty crop. Grossly overdue, but miraculously just in time.

Chapter 6

STOP THE SINGLE STORY (KHADIJAH, RASHEED, AND JAMILA)

An enemy is a person whose story you have not yet heard.
—Slavoj Žižek

"Which of these three, do you think, was a neighbor to the man who fell into the hands of the robbers?" He said, "The one who showed him mercy." Jesus said to him, "Go and do likewise."
—Luke 10:36–37, the Good Samaritan parable

In the powerful, popular TED Talk "The Danger of the Single Story," the Nigerian Catholic author Chimamanda Ngozi Adichie recounts a childhood memory of Fide, her family's houseboy. Growing up, the only thing Adichie ever heard about Fide was how poor he was. Then one day she went to visit Fide's family in his village. Fide's brother showed them a beautiful and ornate basket that he had made. Adichie was shocked. It had not occurred to her that anyone in his family could make anything. "All I had heard about them was how poor they were, so that it had become impossible for me to see them as anything else but poor. Their poverty was my single story of them."[1]

Adichie terms this the danger of the single story and asks, "Have you ever been the victim of a single story told about you?" She laments that when we tell only one story over and over about a person or group, then they become nothing more than a stereotype. The single story is a political tool used by the powerful to otherize certain people and prevent us from forging connections with them as human equals. Adichie ends her TED Talk with an urgent plea to remember that every person, group, and nation has not one story but many.

When someone says the word *Muslim*, what pops into your head? ISIS? Terrorist? Enemy? A Christian student in one of my religion classes once declared: "Islam is a religion of hate. Muslims don't worship the same God, and they don't believe in Jesus." My student is not alone in his views. A majority of Americans—56 percent, to be precise—believe that Islam's values are at odds with American values.[2] In 2017, the president of the United States signed an executive order banning Muslims from seven different predominantly Muslim nations from entering our country.

Arguably, the single story being told about Muslims in our country is that they are all Middle Eastern terrorists—all dangerous members of ISIS who hate Christians and want to destroy the American way of life. Countless Americans—most of them Christians—subscribe to this single story even though seven in ten Americans report that they have seldom or never had a conversation with anyone who is Muslim. (And even though only 20 percent of the world's Muslims actually live in the Middle East.) Let there be no doubt: many consider Muslims the greatest enemy of our times. In such a climate, loving our Muslim neighbors pushes some folks' *agape* to its outermost limits.

A long time ago, I too would have agreed with the single story about Islam. No one can deny that extremists perpetrate horrific, unacceptable acts in the name of Islam (as they do in every religion). But I have come to see there is much more to the story. As part of my classes, my students and I regularly partner with a local Christian social service organization to befriend local refugee and immigrant families. Through that work, my studies, and seven years spent directing my college's interfaith center, I've been blessed with a lot of Muslim friends. These friends have taught me a lot about their faith. And they've also helped me to become a much better Christian. Let me introduce you to a few of them.

Khadijah

Meet Khadijah, her sister Lina, and their parents Karim and Daneen. They are Muslims from Iraq who were relocated by a faith-based refugee resettlement organization to Fargo, North Dakota. About fifteen years ago, Saddam Hussein murdered Khadijah's innocent teenage sister for her political and social views. Khadijah and her family fled their country in the middle of the night, with nothing but the clothes they were wearing. Karim left behind his successful clothing shop, the family business. They lived in a refugee camp in Jordan for seven years, until the vetting process was complete and the United States at last accepted them as political refugees.

I remember the first time my students and I went to Khadijah's house. None of them spoke much English, so we got by with smiles, laughter, one-word declarations, and our own crazy version of charades. "Muslim," Karim said, pointing to his chest. Then he pointed at us. "Jesus? Christian?"

"Yes!" We said, "We're Christians!"

Hearing this, Karim brought his two index fingers from each hand together and announced gleefully, "Very good. We are cousins!"

One day when the family was telling me their story, Karim whipped out his cell phone to show me photos of their former home in Iraq. It was beautiful and spacious, surrounded by lush trees blooming with oranges and lemons. Daneen's eyes pooled with tears. She peered at the cell phone screen as if her entire life had disappeared into it. She, like me, probably couldn't help but compare their Iraq home to the cramped two-bedroom apartment where they now lived, surrounded by snow, in a not-so-beautiful part of Fargo. Before living in Fargo, they had they never seen snow, let alone owned a winter coat. I asked them what had happened to their house in Baghdad. They showed me another photo—it was their house bombed to rubble during our war with Iraq.

Because refugee camps don't provide school transcripts, and the US education bureaucracy requires them, Khadijah is currently being forced to repeat nearly all the years of school she did in Jordan. Even though she's nineteen, she sits all day in a classroom with fourteen- and fifteen-year-olds. "It's so boring!" she tells me, laughing even though I know she's serious.

One day she showed me a paper she wrote for school. She wrote how terrified she was to come to America, because all she had ever seen were American soldiers who carried guns and bombed places where people she loved lived. All she had ever heard was that Americans hate Muslims (Iraq's version of the single story). But then when Khadijah got to America, she was astonished because, "Everyone is so nice!"

Khadijah, in addition to being in school, also works a forty-hour-a-week job and, along with her sister, supports the entire family. Both Khadijah and Lina have to work because their parents' health is failing, and also because they've learned English much faster than them. The stress of losing his home, child, and homeland caused Karim to have a heart attack his first year in the United States.

Once, when Khadijah was working the cash register at Target, a man noticed her hijab (headscarf). "Are you Muslim?" he asked.

"Yes," she said.

"You should go back where you came from," he said, and stalked out. He did not know that right after the terrorist attacks in Paris, Khadijah, like so many Muslims, had changed her Facebook profile picture to the French flag to show solidarity with the victims. Little did he know that I once heard Khadijah agree with a friend who said, "Those planes were not the only thing hijacked on 9/11. My faith was hijacked as well."

My husband and I visit Khadijah's family regularly. The last time we visited, Daneen made a huge, delicious meal. She served Matt and me all the best parts of the duck. The whole family waited until we had had seconds before any of them took anymore themselves. When we left their house, they filled our arms with fruit and candy, even though just a few hours before, Khadijah admitted that she didn't get to have a birthday party this year, because there was "no money." As we went out the door, Karim hugged us and declared, "You are family."

Rasheed

Rasheed was my first Muslim friend. He was Palestinian. We met in my English literature class in my first semester of graduate school. Rasheed and I didn't talk a lot about religion, but we talked nonstop about our mothers and our shared adoration for Toni Morrison.

I was a hot mess that semester, but Rasheed never seemed to mind. After two years spent living at home in Florida where I helped care for my mom, now suddenly I was a thousand miles away trying to earn a master's degree in Connecticut. Every day, a part of me fantasized about quitting school and rushing home to brush my mother's hair or make her breakfast. When I confessed this to Rasheed, he shared that he too had made the tough decision to leave his mom behind and pursue grad school. His mom was a widow who lived alone on the other side of the world. Looking back on it now, it's no wonder Rasheed and I became fast friends.

For Christmas break that first year of grad school, more than anything I wanted to go home and be with my mom and my sister, niece, and nephew. But I was dead broke. I was paying for grad school entirely out of my own pocket, and though I had received a scholarship, it wasn't enough to cover a plane ticket to Florida.

Over lattes one day at our favorite coffee shop, I mentioned my sadness to Rasheed, and joked that I could only afford half of a plane ticket to Florida. My friend listened thoughtfully. Rasheed couldn't afford to fly home either for the holidays, so he was planning on staying in town and working, as well as spending time with a nearby cousin.

"I have an idea," Rasheed said, suddenly inspired. "I have three days off work during break. How about I drive you home and then you buy a one-way ticket back?"

"Rasheed, you *do* get that my house is literally a thousand miles from here?" I asked.

"Of course I do," he replied. "But every mile will be worth it the second you step out of the car and I see the look on your mom's face."

(These days, whenever I hear someone say something single-story-bad about Muslims, I'm overcome with an urge to shove them into a time machine, and *Back-to-the-Future* their ass straight into that moment.)

Rasheed wasn't kidding around. A few days later, we packed our bags and we left. At one point during the roadtrip, I spun the radio dial and stumbled across some Christmas music. I stopped for a minute to listen, but then quickly switched the station.

"Hey, why'd you change that?" Rasheed asked. "I liked that song!" I told him I assumed that because he was Muslim, he wouldn't be down with Jesus-music like *It Came Upon a Midnight Clear*.

Rasheed said, "Where'd you get that idea? I love Jesus." I laughed. Then, to make me laugh even harder, he rolled down his window and bellowed into the frosty air of the New Jersey Turnpike, "I LOVE JESUS!"

As we drove, Rasheed explained that Jesus is a beloved prophet within Islam (though not the son of God) and also that the Qur'an says Jesus was born of a virgin named Mary. Only if Rasheed had turned out to be Santa Claus could I have been more stunned. Clearly, I was clueless about my friend's religion.

Finally, after a seventeen-hour drive, we arrived at my house in Florida. Rasheed smiled as he watched me hug my mother. Then he quickly used the bathroom, climbed back into his car, and retraced the same thousand miles back to his Connecticut dorm.

After graduate school, Rasheed and I stayed in touch. But shortly after September 11, 2001, my emails to him bounced back. I heard through the grapevine that Rasheed had lost his visa and was deported. Like many Muslims post-9/11, he was assumed to be the enemy.

I never heard from Rasheed again, but he changed my life and heart forever.

Because of Rasheed, I went on to study—and now teach—Islam. Thanks to him, my knowledge has traveled miles beyond the Jersey Turnpike. For instance, I've learned that many Muslims actually do love Jesus. Amani Al-Khatahtbeh, the founder of the number one Muslim women's blog in the United States (Muslimgirl.com), recounts in her memoir *Muslim Girl* her father's words, "We love Jesus, too. People should know that."[3] But most non-Muslims, especially Christians, don't know this.

This year, my wonderful Muslim friend Fauzia was the first person to reach out and wish me a Merry Christmas on December 25. (By the way, virtually none of my Christian friends did so.) I thanked her, then asked her if I could interview her for this chapter. Generously, she said yes and had this to say about Christmas:

When I wish my Christian friends and neighbors *Merry Christmas*, I'm sharing in their celebration and joy. . . . Some of my Muslim friends have Christmas trees in their homes and get gifts for the kids, too. I buy Christmas gifts for my Christian friends, coworkers, and children's teachers. . . . Some people believe that celebrating other faith's customs and traditions will weaken their own faith, but . . . in my own opinion that means their faith is weak, not strong. Being a Muslim who celebrates other faith's customs and traditions and learns about other faiths has helped me learn more about my own faith. . . . It has helped me become a better Muslim. So *Merry Christmas* my friend!

Sadly, most Americans don't know Fauzia or Rasheed, and don't know anything about Islam other than what we see on the media, which almost exclusively covers extremist Muslims who do atrocious things in the name of their religion. There are 1.6 billion Muslims in the world, living on all continents. To think that they all belong to—or even agree with—ISIS or the Taliban is as outlandish as assuming that all Christians belong to the Ku Klux Klan or Westboro Baptist Church. If you want to find out what Muslims really believe, read the fascinating results of the latest global Gallup poll, *Who Speaks for Islam? What a Billion Muslims Really Think.* But in the meantime, here's my short version of Islam 101.

When I give talks on Islam in classrooms, churches, and communities, I start with a ten-question literacy survey I designed. It's a basic starting tool for helping folks separate fact from fiction when it comes to Islam. (The average score of the people who take this survey is three or four questions correct out of ten, which of course is an F—surely a consequence of the single story.) One survey question is: How many times does the Qur'an, the sacred text of Islam, mention Jesus? This question trips most people up. What would you answer? Never? Twice? Fifteen times? Fifty times? Answer: the Qur'an mentions Jesus in ninety-three different verses. This is vastly more times than even Muhammad, the prophet to whom Muslims believe the Qur'an was revealed, who only gets five mentions by name.

Most Christians are aware that Muhammad is an incredibly important prophet and teacher within Islam, but very few realize Jesus is too. Far too many Christians have no clue Jesus appears in the Qur'an at all, let alone in such a favorable light. Yet, here's what Fauzia had to say about Jesus, "If I don't believe in Jesus or any of the other prophets and their holy books, then I am not a Muslim. Whenever people in the West insult Prophet Muhammad, I always think: I could never do that to Jesus, because he is my prophet too!"

The Qur'an also refers to Jesus by many other honorable names Christians would recognize, including Christ, Messiah, and Word of God. For example, "Behold! the angels said: 'O Mary! God giveth thee glad tidings of a Word from Him: his name will be Christ Jesus, the son of Mary, held in honour in this world and the Hereafter and of (the company of) those nearest to God'" (Q. 3:45).

The Qur'an teaches not only that Jesus was the son of Mary (as you see in the above verse) but also that Mary was a virgin. In fact, the virgin Mary is the only woman mentioned by name in the Qur'an, which devotes an entire chapter to her. The Qur'an states that Jesus was without sin, and that he healed the sick and performed miracles. "He [Jesus] will be a Messenger of God to the Israelites to whom he will say, 'I have brought you a miracle from your Lord. . . . I can heal the blind and the lepers and bring the dead back to life, by the permission of God'" (Q. 3:49). Additionally, Muslims believe in the second coming of Jesus—that Jesus will come again to judge the living and the dead at the end of time.

Almost none of my students are aware of these similarities between Christianity and Islam when they first step into my classroom. They are as shocked as I once was when they first pick up the Qur'an and realize that virtually all the players—Adam, Eve, Abraham, Moses, the angel Gabriel, Hagar, Isaac, Ishmael, Joseph,

Jesus, Mary—are the exact same as the Bible. Even many of the stories about these folks are similar: Joseph gets thrown in a well by his jealous brothers and sold into slavery; God asks Abraham to sacrifice his son; the angel Gabriel tells the virgin Mary she will have a child; and so on.

Though a vast number of Christians assume the Qur'an negates the Bible, in fact much of the Qur'an presupposes and builds upon it. Remember Ishmael in the Bible, the boy Abraham conceived with the servant Hagar when Sarah couldn't have a baby? Well, many denominations of Islam teach that Ishmael was one of prophet Muhammad's ancestors. Think of it this way: while Christians and Jews trace their family tree back to Abraham and Sarah's son Isaac, Muslims trace their family tree back to Abraham and Hagar's son, Ishmael. (That's why my friend Karim referred to Christians and Muslims as cousins. If you go all the way back to the beginning with Abraham, we're all related!) And here's how Fauzia expressed it, "My faith is incomplete without all the other Abrahamic faiths. They are all part of one whole."

The Bible doesn't have a whole lot to say about Ishmael, but what it does say is significant. Genesis reports that God declared: "As for Ishmael, I have heard you; I will bless him and make him fruitful and exceedingly numerous; he shall be the father of twelve princes, and I will make him a great nation" (17:20). The Bible stops there and never tells what happened to Ishmael and the nation God made of him in the desert of the Middle East. Who are these people to whom God refers in Genesis? They're clearly not Isaac's lineage—those folks became the nation of Israel. For many Christian and Muslim interpreters alike, this verse refers to Muslims, for they are the ones who trace their lineage back to Ishmael and Hagar. Who else could that nation be? If it's Muslims, it's important to note the Bible says (a) God *made* them a nation and (b) God *blesses* them.

The Qur'an picks up our cousins' story where the Bible leaves off. What many Christians find scandalous, however, is the fact that in places, the Qur'an goes beyond elaboration of the Bible and instead modifies or omits parts of it. Many years ago, I felt puzzled and put-off by this, until I realized that my own tradition of Christianity had done the exact same thing to the Jewish Bible (which Christians call the Old Testament).

I mean, how many times does Jesus say in the New Testament, "You have heard it said X, but I say to you, Y" (e.g., Matthew 5:43–44)? A lot! Every time Jesus says something like that, he's criticizing, contradicting, and/or reforming his Jewish tradition. I had never stopped to care how this made my Jewish brothers and sisters feel. An important part of my holy text—the so-called New Testament—constantly "corrects" and adds to the Jewish scriptures; indeed, my Christian tradition actually folds the Jewish tradition into its own Bible and calls it old! (Many of my Jewish friends actually do find this hurtful, and prefer Christians call the Old Testament by its right name, the Hebrew Bible or *Tanakh*).

For all these reasons, it blew my mind when my Muslim friend Ahmad once noted, "Jacqueline, Christians added the 'new' testament to the original Jewish scriptures, right? Christians understand the New Testament to be God's new revelation to the world, through Jesus. Well, Muslims see the Qur'an the same way. God has also given us a new revelation, through Muhammad. To us, the Qur'an is the *new* New Testament." Ahmad pointed me toward verse 29:46 in the Qur'an: "And do not argue with the People of the Scripture except in a way that is best, except for those who commit injustice among them, and say, 'We believe in that which has been revealed to us and revealed to you. And our God and your God is one; and we are Muslims [in submission] to Him.'"

A quick clarification about the phrase "People of the Scripture," usually translated "People of the Book." A lot of Christians who pick up the Qur'an don't understand that this refers to them, to both Christians and Jews. Instead, they think the Qur'an's term *unbeliever* applies to them. But remember that Bible—*biblia*—literally means *books*. People of the Book = People of the Bible! The Qur'an does not refer to Christians and Jews as unbelievers, as the single story would have you believe; no, they're People of the Book. Many Christians may believe all Muslims are unbelievers across the board, but it's important to know the reverse is not the case. When I asked Fauzia about this, she said, "I don't see Christians as 'others,' but instead as People of the Book with whom I share my faith tradition."

Contrary to popular opinion, the Qur'an does not dispute the overall legitimacy of the Bible or its status as God's word and revelation to Jews and Christians. On the contrary, Qur'an 3:84 states, "We believe in God and in that which has been revealed to us and in that which was revealed to Abraham, Ishmael, Isaac, Jacob, and their descendants. We believe in that which was given to Moses, Jesus, and the Prophets by their Lord. We make no distinction between them and we have submitted ourselves to the will of God."

Of course, everything is not peaches and cream. In addition to these surprising similarities between Christianity and Islam, important differences also exist. Especially with regard to Jesus. Interfaith dialogue should never deny or gloss over these distinctions. For example, Islam, unlike Christianity, does not teach that Jesus was divine, or the Son of God. In Islam, Jesus is a prophet, a very special, sinless prophet born of a virgin, but still only a human. Perhaps most worrisome to Christians, one passage in the Qur'an seems to suggest that although people *believed* Jesus was crucified, God actually took his soul straight to heaven (though Muslim scholars dispute the precise interpretation of this verse). What's clear in any case is that Muslims do not believe that Jesus is a savior or God incarnate in the sense that Christians do.

Again, these differences matter. A lot (and for some people more than others). What's troubling though is the fact that they are the single story, leaving many Christians with no shared humanity upon which to extend *agape*-love to their Muslim neighbors. The single story is a political tool, used by people in every religion, to divide and recruit people to hate or violence. If you don't believe me, just ask ISIS.

I once heard a Christian theologian say, "Christians do not own Jesus." This thought discomfits many Christians. But it shouldn't. Isn't it true that Jesus has to be infinitely bigger than any Tupperware we want to shove him in? Isn't it better that people of other religions come to know, respect, and love Jesus, rather than not know him at all?

Can those who claim to be followers of Jesus seriously prefer that folks of other religions have *no* relationship with him, unless it is on our terms? I can't in good conscience prefer this. I want everyone to know Jesus because he is wondrous and his love takes my breath away. And hey, let's be real: even the scriptures reject the idea of a single story when it comes to Jesus. That's why the Bible has four Gospels rather than one.

What about the claim that Muslims worship a different God than Christians, a god called Allah? When I was in Jerusalem, I worshiped at a Christian church where the service was in Arabic and English. The Christians in the pews next to me were Arab, and so spoke Arabic. Guess what those Arabic-speaking Christians called God every time they prayed, sang, and said the creeds in church? Allah. And guess what their Christian Bible, written in Arabic, called God? That's right, Allah. In the exact same way that Christians who speak Spanish call God *Dios*, Christians who speak Arabic call God *Allah*. There is no other word for God in Arabic. (Note: this paragraph is another passage that my original Christian publisher asked me to delete. Hmmm . . . was this because its contents threatened to spoil the single story?)

Language aside, many Christians still deny that Muslims worship the same God as them. Some argue that Muslims don't worship the same God because they don't believe Jesus is their savior. Others argue that the God of the Qur'an is violent and nasty, unlike the loving God of the Bible. Yes, the Qur'an condones violence in some sections, especially in self-defense, but it also says regarding enemies, "If they leave you alone and do not fight you and offer you peace, then God allows you no way against them." (Q. 4:90)

Moreover, the God of the Bible also encourages violence. Exodus 15:3 states, "The Lord is a warrior." And in Deuteronomy 13:6–10, God commands believers to kill: "If anyone secretly entices you—even if it is your brother, your father's son or your mother's son, or your own son or daughter, or the wife you embrace, or your most intimate friend—saying, 'Let us go worship other gods.' . . . But you shall surely kill them; your own hand shall be first against them to execute them, and afterwards the hand of all the people. Stone them to death for trying to turn you away from the Lord your God." Or what about the time Jesus said, "Do not think that I have come to bring peace to the earth; I have not come to bring peace, but a sword" (Matthew 10:34)? Imagine how menacing these biblical passages might sound to our interfaith neighbors when cherry-picked out of context, the way Christians often quote troubling passages from the Qur'an!

Most Muslims, in contrast, *do* believe they worship the exact same God as Christians and Jews. The Bible states that the God whom Jews and Christians worship is the God of Abraham, Isaac, and Jacob (Exodus 3:15). Likewise Muslims, according to the Qur'an, worship the God of Abraham, Isaac, and Jacob (Q. 12:38). The Qur'an refers to Abraham as the father of Muslims (Q. 22:78) The faithful in all three religions—Judaism, Christianity, and Islam—claim to worship the God of Abraham. Once more, here's how my friend Fauzia summed it up, "I was taught that Islam is the latest edition of the Abrahamic faiths. It's a continuation of them, not a new faith."

This raises a related question. Do mainstream Christians believe that they worship the same God as Jews? Absolutely, yes, this is the official teaching of Christianity. Nearly all Christians believe this in spite of the fact that Jews, like Muslims, do not consider Jesus to be divine or the messiah. This is a double standard. How would those of us who are Christians feel if our Jewish brothers and sisters said, "Jesus-freaks, we don't believe in Jesus like you do, so there's no way you're worshipping the God of Abraham, Isaac, and Jacob like we are. Stop stealing our Bible and adding stuff to it!!"

Fortunately, our Jewish brothers and sisters don't say this, but instead graciously accept that we are worshipping the God of Israel, whom they believe is the God of *all* people and not only of themselves. If Christians get to decide that they're worshipping the same God of Abraham as the Jews, why can't Muslims claim the same thing? This double standard is another example of anemic *agape*.

Jamila

Let me introduce you to one last Muslim friend of mine, Jamila.

Jamila, who was born in the United States and is a nurse at our local hospital, came to visit my interfaith studies class. She graciously told my students that no questions were off limits. One of my students asked her what favorite quote was in the Qur'an or in the *hadith* (the book of sayings and stories about the prophet Muhammad). She took our breath away by sharing this saying, in which Muslims understand God to be speaking to human beings: "When anyone comes towards me a hand's breadth, I approach a forearm's length; if anyone comes towards me a forearm's length, I approach by the space of outstretched arms; if anyone comes toward me walking, I will come running. Then I love that person so that I become the eyes with which he sees, the ears with which he hears, the hands with which he takes hold. And should that person bring to me sins the size of the earth, my forgiveness will be a match for them."[4]

One of my evangelical students, Kris, asked Jamila why she chose to wear a hijab (a head-scarf that covers the hair and neck, not to be confused with the burka, which covers the whole body and face). Jamila said, "Every Muslim woman wears the hijab for her own reasons. No one tells me I have to wear hijab; I choose to. The Qur'an doesn't say women have to cover their heads, but it instructs us to be modest. I choose to wear the hijab for modesty. And also, because I'm a feminist. As a woman, I don't want to be judged by my looks or by the size of my chest, I want to be judged by my character and my actions."

Nearly everyone in the room was wowed by this answer. My progressive Christian students were amazed to hear a Muslim woman describe the hijab as a symbol of women's equality. As for the evangelical Christian students, Kris remarked that her own parents had always taught her to dress modestly, for the exact same reasons (minus the feminist part). Kris talked about the pressure on women in our society to be bone thin and to dress in skinny jeans, skimpy bikinis, and low-cut tank tops. Then Kris showed us this burka versus bikini political cartoon,[5] which made us all pretty uneasy.

After a few minutes of looking at the cartoon, several students observed that though many of us righteously believe that our own culture is exempt from upholding standards that hurt women, perhaps that is yet another single story we tell ourselves.

Jamila then added, "You know what's weird? The only time people judge a head-covering as oppressive is when it's on top of a Muslim woman's head; never when it's on top of a nun's." One of my students went to the classroom computer and called up a picture of Mother Teresa on Google images. When Mother Teresa appeared on the overhead screen, sporting her usual blue and white headscarf, my students gasped. One of them said, "Why had I never noticed this before? Her scarf looks exactly like a hijab!" Two students then did a short role play in which one person complained that Islam was oppressive because many Muslim women cover their heads. My student Luke jokingly countered, "Um, well. Nuns exist." The class—rightly—laughed hard at this.

Once they settled down, I shared with them that the religious idea of head-covering originally comes not from Islam but—surprise!—from the Bible. And not the Old Testament but the New! Specifically 1 Corinthians 11:5–6: "Any woman who prays or prophesies with her head unveiled disgraces her head. . . . For if a woman will not veil herself, then she should cut off her hair; but if it is disgraceful for a woman to have her hair cut off or to be shaved, she should wear a veil." I also informed them of a group of Christian women who recently started a movement to cover their heads in light of this verse.[6]

As a class, we concluded that an aspect of the single story being told today about Islam is that it oppresses women. In some countries, yes, Islam is indeed manipulated by patriarchal men to abuse and disenfranchise women. Of course, in some parts of the world and even in some households right here in the United States, men use Christianity in exactly the same way. (Author and pastor Rob Bell, for example, recounts the disturbing story of a young woman whose father molested her while reciting the Lord's Prayer.[7]) We should reject and resist all actions that oppress women, regardless of who commits them.

Not all predominantly Christian nations in the world treat women the same way; some, like Ethiopia and Eritrea, practice female genital mutilation. Similarly, there are thirty-five predominantly Muslim nations in the world, and they don't all treat women the same way. Five predominantly Muslim countries in the world have democratically elected a woman to be head of state (president or prime minister), while our own country has never yet done so.[8] If this fact astonishes you, remember the danger of a single story—it coerces you to believe that certain people are unable to be or create anything beautiful, true, or good. I don't know about you, but I'm sick and tired of people and politicians trying to sucker me into signing on to a single story—about anyone.

Were you aware of the hundreds of Muslims in Lahore, Pakistan, on Sunday, October 6, 2013, who formed a human chain around a Christian church? Concerned about recent terrorist attacks on minorities in their country, these Muslims formed the chain so that their Christian brothers and sisters could worship safely and without fear. In their hands they carried a huge banner that read "One Nation, One Blood."[9] It's a fact, and you can see the pictures online, but did it make your nightly news? Did you hear about the Muslims in my hometown of Jacksonville, Florida, who opened up a free health clinic where top-notch Muslim doctors provide health care to thousands of patients absolutely free?[10] No? See—single story.

I'm fed up with love losing to the single story. In troubled times like ours, those who follow Jesus must trounce the single story. The simplest way to do this is to befriend people who are stereotyped by it. Prominent Christian pastor Brian McLaren writes,

Imagine what might happen around the world if more and more Christians rediscover that central to Christian life and mission is what we could call subversive or transgressive friendship—friendship that crosses boundaries of otherness and dares to offer and receive hospitality. . . . Imagine the good that could happen—and the evil that could be prevented from happening—if more Jews, Muslims, Hindus, Christians, Buddhists and others cross the roads and other barriers that have separated them, and discover one another as friends.[11]

I believe McLaren is right: in a world of hate and horrifying headlines, transgressive friendships can change hearts. I know, because it's the only thing that's ever changed mine.

Christians are called to forge transgressive friendships because Jesus was the absolute maestro of transgressive friendship. Jesus palled around with everyone he was told not to—tax collectors, prostitutes, lepers, poor people, sick people. What would Jesus say to us today about our Muslim neighbors? The parable of the Good Samaritan provides an answer (Luke 10).

We all know the story. A lawyer, eager to condemn Jesus, asks Jesus, "Who is my neighbor?" Jesus then tells the story of a Jewish man who lay beaten in the ditch. Two fine upstanding Jewish guys walked past—one of them a priest and the other a Levite—but neither stopped. Only a Samaritan stopped to help. We don't have a clue what this story means unless we know who the Samaritans were to Jesus' listeners: Samaritans were the enemy. For example, in one Gospel, the people insult Jesus by labeling him a demon-possessed Samaritan (John 8:48).

When I was young and heard this passage read in church, I always assumed the Jews and Samaritans were enemies because they differed in nationality or race. Incorrect. The animosity between Jews and Samaritans was over *religion*. Virtually all of Jesus' Jewish community believed the Samaritans practiced a false faith. It's not that the Samaritans were pagans or idol-worshippers. No, they worshipped the God of Abraham, Isaac, and Jacob exactly like the Jews. The problem was that in the fourth century BCE, the Samaritans scandalously built on Mount Gerizim the only temple that ever rivaled the Jerusalem temple. Writes one biblical scholar, "The mutually exclusive claims of Gerizim and Jerusalem as the most sacred place in the world constitute the most distinctive difference between Jew and Samaritan."[12] Makes you wonder if two thousand years from now, people will have forgotten the reasons why people of different religions hated each other the same way most of us have forgotten this one.

In seminary, I was shocked to learn that Samaritans survive today, and they live in the holy land. Equally surprising: some Palestinian Muslims alive today are understood to be converted descendants from the original Samaritans.

In my view, the Good Samaritan parable is Jesus' first-century Palestinian version of Adichie's "Danger of a Single Story" TED Talk. By telling a new story with a Samaritan as the hero, Jesus slayed the single story his society subscribed to about Samaritans. He scandalized and offended his audience. That shock is lost on twenty-first-century Christians, unless we retell the story in contemporary terms, like this.

A twenty-first-century Christian approached Jesus and asked, "Who is my neighbor?" And Jesus answered: "There was a Christian man on his way across the city of Detroit to feed the homeless. On his way there, a street gang mugged him and beat him senseless, leaving him in the gutter to die.

A pastor walked by on the street and, seeing the bloodied man in the gutter, crossed to the other side of the street, thinking, *please don't let that homeless guy make eye contact with me*. A few minutes later, a Christian woman who was the president of her church congregation walked past. She too crossed to the other side of the street thinking, *look at that guy, probably a crack addict or a drunk.*

And then a Muslim man walked by, saw the man lying in the gutter, and stopped. Moved with compassion he said, 'My friend, let me take you to the ER.' Once at the hospital, the Muslim man realized the beat-up guy didn't have health care. 'That's okay, I'll pay,' he told the nurse at check-in and paid two days of his entire salary for the care of this man whose name he didn't even know. Even though he had to go to work the next day, the Muslim man decided to sit at the man's bedside all night, so he wouldn't feel alone or afraid if he woke up.

In the morning, when the Muslim left, he gave the hospital his cell number and said, 'If the man in room 109 incurs any more charges, call me and I'll cover those as well.'

Those who have ears to hear, go and do likewise."

Whenever I preach on the Samaritan parable, I share this rewritten version. Without fail, people squirm in the pews. I take this to mean my retelling helps us to feel in our bones once again the radical nature of Jesus' call to love without limits. It certainly helps remind me why lots of religious folks wanted to crucify Jesus.

Who have you been taught to believe is your "Samaritan" neighbor of a "bad" religion? We could substitute virtually any faith or philosophy—Buddhist, Hindu, Jewish, Sikh, Christian, or atheist—for Muslim in our retelling, because sadly, almost every religion has practitioners who demonize folks of other faiths.

The Samaritan in Jesus' original parable is the true neighbor. He is a human who sees other humans, no matter their religion, as beloved children of God, worthy of mercy and care. The Samaritan doesn't attempt to convert the injured man to his faith, either before or after providing help. Instead, the Samaritan demonstrates through actions alone the supersize love his faith commands of him. Jesus points at this man and says to all of us: *hey, get out there and act just like this guy.*

The Good Samaritan parable is a summons to interfaith friendship, cooperation, care, and mercy. In telling it, Jesus calls us to reject with a resounding NO the single stories that we have heard about people of other faiths. He provides a radical three-part solution to the hate and violence of our religiously diverse world.

1. Get to know your neighbors of other faiths. Act with measureless love toward them.
2. Reject cultural and political messages of fear; instead, believe in the goodness and kindness of your neighbors of other faiths.
3. Understand that folks of other religions have something valuable to teach you.

The theologian Krister Stendahl had three great rules for interfaith understanding that are similar to Jesus'.

1. When trying to understand another faith, ask the adherents of that faith and not its critics or enemies.
2. Don't compare your best to their worst.
3. Leave room for "holy envy"—meaning, that idea or practice that another faith has that you admire, appreciate, and want to have more of in your own faith.[13]

In keeping with both #3s, I want to end this chapter by sharing with you a moment of holy envy and some things I've learned from my Muslim friends that have deepened my own faith as a Christian.

Arabic is the original language of the Qur'an, and Muslims consider it a sacred language. In Arabic, the word for *human being* means *one who forgets*. In this understanding, the most essential thing about humans is that we forget. We forget everything— the poor, God, each other. Therefore, we must constantly be reminded. Once I understood this about Islam, so much of the religion clicked.

Consider Ramadan, the Muslim practice of fasting for forty days. I asked several Muslim friends why they fast on Ramadan, and they said, "By feeling the pains of hunger in our stomachs every day, we remember the poor and what it feels like to go hungry. We remember that God calls us to give to them and to strive to correct systems that keep people in poverty. Without Ramadan, we might forget this." Likewise, consider the Muslim practice of praying five times a day facing the holy city of Mecca. This is how many Muslims take a few intentional minutes every day to remember God and God's compassion and mercy.

Recently, my students and I were invited to the Muslim country of Oman in the Middle East to engage in Christian-Muslim dialogue. I had never before been in a Muslim country. Every day, five times a day, the call to prayer sang out over the entire town, broadcast live through a loudspeaker atop the local mosque. I was surprised to see that most Muslims stopped whatever they were doing to heed this call to pray. Cars pulled over to the side of the road. Shopkeepers walked away from clients. Students stepped out of class. When I traveled with Muslim friends to remote or rural places where the call to prayer could not be heard, they used an app called Muslim Pro on their phones to tell them when to pray.

My first morning in Oman, a little before dawn, I was awakened by the morning call to prayer. It was louder than any alarm clock and impossible to sleep through. I was annoyed and exhausted. I lay in bed jet-lagged and frustrated, while my Muslim hosts pulled themselves away from their pillows to pray.

But on the third morning, as I lay awake at 5:00 a.m. listening to the *adhan*, my spirit awakened to a humbling realization. My Muslim brothers and sisters prioritized remembering God over everything, even sleep. Would I be willing to do the same? Suddenly, I felt not irritation but admiration. I structure my prayers around my life, while my Muslim friends do the exact opposite. They structure their entire lives around prayer.

105

This deep devotion inspired holy envy in me as a Christian. To this day, whenever I wake up in the early morning or middle of the night, instead of feeling frustrated at sleep's elusiveness, I try to pray. Often my prayer sounds something like this. *Love, never stop showing me how much I have left to learn.*

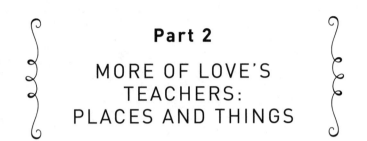

Part 2

MORE OF LOVE'S TEACHERS: PLACES AND THINGS

Chapter 7

CAN ANYTHING GOOD COME OUT OF NAZARETH? (FARGO)

Perhaps I will stay with you or even spend the winter,
so that you may send me on my way, wherever I go.
—1 Corinthians 16:6

Birds that migrate or winter hundreds of miles outside their familiar territory are called *vagrants*. Most people who grow up in Fargo, North Dakota, migrate in their retirement to Florida. I, on the other hand, grew up in Florida and now live in Fargo. I've always been a strange bird, but—even for me—this vagrancy breaks records. It's official: I've lived my life backward.

What does the name Fargo make you think of? An uninhabitable wasteland? A wintry void? Yeah, that's how I always imagined Fargo too. Not because I'd ever visited there or known anyone from there, but because I, like most Americans, let the popular Coen brothers' 1996 movie *Fargo* tell me everything I needed to know. For all who've seen this gloomy satirical film or its spin-off TV series of the same name, Fargo conjures up images of rural

America at its worst—lawless, dreary, corrupt, grotesque, and ignorant. In the film's most unforgettable scene, a conscienceless criminal stuffs his murder victim into a woodchipper. In our popular imagination, Fargo = Nowheresville. The place no one wants to live, filled with people no one wants to meet. Turns out, even places have a single story.

No one loves summer and sun more than the woman typing these words. I mean seriously, it's like a sickness. What am I saying? It *is* a sickness. I suffer from seasonal affective disorder. So in 2010, when a headhunter from Concordia College in Fargo's neighboring city Moorhead, Minnesota, approached me about applying for the new position of director of the Forum on Faith and Life, I replied with a polite, "No way." The job was a huge promotion and sounded fascinating, but still, I declined. Any normal person would, right?

As if my *No!* got drowned out by the Great Plains' forty-five-mile-an-hour wind gusts, the chair of the search committee kept calling back anyway. For nine months. "Don't make me do this," I begged God in my prayers. "Please, no. Anywhere but there."

Finally, I could no longer ignore the obvious. The position was the dream job I'd waited for my whole life. My life was an email, and God was pressing send. I moved to Fargo. Kicking and screaming and scared out of my suntanned wits. I know it sounds ridiculous to say that I was afraid of weather—of winter—but I was. Seven months of winter is a long time, in a year only twelve months long.

I never used to think of *agape*-love as something I needed to extend toward a place or a season, but Fargo has taught me that to do so is a spiritual necessity. In spite of myself, Fargo has lifted my understanding of radical love to a whole new latitude. Here's some of her best wisdom.

Fargo's Five Love Lessons

Fargo Lesson One:
Comparison Is the Root of Unhappiness. Love Yourself Enough
to Stop Already

My first winter in Fargo, my fascinated friends and family in Florida frequently called to see how I was surviving. Cocooned in my indoor igloo of heated blankets, I fielded questions such as: Had my eyelashes frozen shut yet? Was it still fifty below zero? How many times a day did I need to start my car to make sure that the battery wouldn't die? Was it true that if you poured a kettle of boiling water outside, the water would instantly evaporate before even making it to the ground?

One day in the thirtieth month of winter, while answering these questions for my sister—*no, yes, twice, yes!*—I heard a strange noise on the other end of the line. "What's that noise?" I asked.

"What noise?" she asked back.

"That whoosh in the background."

"Oh that," my sister replied breezily. "Wind. I have the window down in my car."

To my poor gelid mind, a rolled-down car window had already become as fantastic as a unicorn.

The image of fresh, clean air blowing across my sister's face—air that would not freeze her nose hairs in an instant—ripped off my blindfold. I was a jealous person—capable of spine-bending, joy-sucking jealousy. Apparently even over the pettiest of things, such as oxygen. I had long prided myself on overcoming my jealous streak. But now I saw that my envy had not died. It had merely gone into remission during the time I possessed the very thing I believed most people wanted: a Florida life. The sound of the ocean in my ears. The sun on my face all year-round. Vitamin D showering down upon me like parade candy. Once geography denied me those things, my green-eyed disease erupted anew. "A heart at peace gives life to the body, but envy rots the bones" (Proverbs 14:30).

After I hung up with my sister, I realized what my mother taught me at age twelve—when I wished I could be a cheerleader rather than a band geek—was absolutely true. "Comparison is the thief of joy," she'd said, quoting Teddy Roosevelt. She knew that if comparison is misery's drug of choice, then an addict's only way out is to cut off its supply.

And so I decided to go cold turkey (pun intended). I began with my phone's weather app, where I went every day to score my daily hit. I had it set to show me not only Fargo's temperature but also the temperature in other places, like Florida (so I could feel miserable, self-pitying, and resentful) and Fairbanks (so I could at least feel better than Alaskans, though this often backfired, sending my misery-meter soaring). But from that day forward, I changed it to show me only one city's weather: Fargo. My new rule of thumb became: never, ever look at the weather for a city in which you do not live. (Concern for others and travel excepted, of course.)

Comparison in any direction whipsaws you with misery—south, with dissatisfaction and inferiority, and north, with snobbishness and superiority. This is why you must stop already, and show yourself some love.

As a kid growing up in Florida, I wore my superiority like a second skin. One January, my Wisconsin cousins came to visit us. For us Sunshine-Staters, it was an exceptionally cold day—around fifty degrees. My cousins swam the afternoon away, while my best friend and I sat inside and mocked them for their blue-lipped joy. Another time in high school I was driving to the beach with friends, and on I-95 we spotted the usual plethora of cars with Ohio license plates. I said to my friends, "Wouldn't it be awful to live in a place you hated so much that you always had to leave it?" My friends and I laughed loudly as we sped past the poor snowbirds on the interstate, exuding deep-fried Southern contempt for their eternal exodus.

Guess where I landed my first university teaching job? In Columbus, *Ohio*. One of the top-ten cloudiest/most overcast cities in the United States. I lived there for eight years, the Divine's sense of humor—or justice—sledgehammering into my soul.

A recent study revealed that the more hours a day kids look at Facebook, the lower they rate their own happiness. The study didn't speculate why, but I'd bet my bottom dollar on comparison. Have you ever looked at friends' pages on Facebook and secretly thought, *Man, why can't I go to Paris for my birthday like them? Why does their kid win all those awards? Gosh darn it, why do they look so happy all the time?* Why, why, why!?!? Before you know it, you've worked yourself into a frenzy of despondency—and hate the very life you cherished ten minutes ago before opening your laptop.

Facebook, though, should really be called *Fakebook*. No one's life is as perfect or pleasant as it looks online. One of my Facebook friends commented, "Jacqueline, I can't even believe your life! All you do is travel the world and have fun!" I joked back that if my life looked glamorous, it was only because I chose *not* to post pictures of myself arguing with my husband, puking into the toilet with stomach flu, tearing my hair out over office politics, or scrubbing shat from my basement floor when the old sewage pipe backed up . . . AGAIN! Most of us don't mean to be fake on Facebook, but, like people on a first date, we do wear only our best outfits.

In contrast, scripture shows people in their sweatpants. Take, for example, Cain and Abel. Genesis straight-up names it: Cain slew Abel because he compared his own life to his brother's, and he felt jealous. "And the Lord had regard for Abel and his offering, but for Cain and his offering he had no regard. So Cain was very angry, and his countenance fell. The Lord said to Cain, 'Why are you angry, and why has your countenance fallen? . . . Sin is lurking at the door; its desire is for you, but you must master it'" (Genesis

4:4–7). Comparison makes us Cains. If social media tortures you, stop being a junkie. Limit your screen time. Or give it up altogether.

Fargo has humbled me and enlarged my *agape*-love to include those it never before did. It's taught me to stop being a snob about things like where a person's birth, calling, or love place them in this world. I get it now. Finally.

Privilege—though a prickly subject—is real, including *weather privilege*. (Yes, even though I made that term up, it's definitely a thing.) Like all privilege, I never noticed mine until it was gone. Like any privilege we refuse to admit exists, mine didn't make me a kinder or better person. Instead, it made me self-righteous about perks I happened to have that other people didn't—such as sunshine and long summers—that I did nothing whatsoever to earn or deserve. Fargo made me see that someday your life's plot may reverse the telescope your eye sees the world through and what was once far-off will startle your retina, if God determines that is what is required.

Take it from this vagrant bird, the Arctic can teach you a lot about *agape*.

Fargo Lesson Two:
Home Is Where Love (Not the Weather) Keeps You Warm

I have never understood why people imagine hell as a hot place. For me, heat is heavenly. I once read that Madonna hates air-conditioning and refuses to turn it on. This is the one thing—probably the only thing—the '80s pop singer and I have in common. You have no idea how much I hate cold and love heat. I mean, seriously. When it's ninety-five degrees outside, I go for three-mile runs, but when I'm in a house where people keep the AC on seventy, I shiver like a shaved cat.

During my first winter in Fargo, the temperature hovered around twenty-five degrees below zero for nearly a month. On days when the wind chill reached fifty below, we were warned not to let pets outdoors, or even to go outside to get the mail. My sister-in-law sent us a plant that Christmas. In the time that it took the UPS driver to walk the twenty yards from his truck to our doorbell, the plant was dead, flash frozen like a Costco blueberry.

Yet, one day that same winter, the unimaginable happened. Fresh from my white-knuckled drive to the college where I work, I was walking down the hall to my office when the first student of the day smiled at me. In spite of myself, I thought: *your calling is what keeps you warm.*

This had always been true, of course. But when I lived somewhere warm, there was no way in my thick-headedness (and thin-skinnedness) that I could have peeled away the rind to reveal this juicy-fruit truth. Now I know. As much as it hurts my ego to admit it, I am happier living in Fargo—the last place in the world I ever wanted to live—than I ever was living most places I've lived in my life.

The sole reason for this is my vocation—my calling. I love the community and students I serve here. In Fargo, I feel valued and respected and, well, needed. Once a student whispered to me on her way out my classroom door, "Please don't ever leave." Meaningful days filled with what novelist Gail Godwin calls "the grace of daily obligation" have always kept me warm, but it took living in the subarctic to make me realize it.

Of course, a lot of the time I'm still too stubborn to admit this. During the next polar vortex, no doubt I'll need you to remind me I ever did.

In my Lutheran tradition (ELCA), soon-to-be pastors (seminarians) fill out a form indicating in which part of the country they'd be willing to serve a congregation. This first position as a pastor after graduation is called *first call*. One of the boxes on the form says: "I am willing to go anywhere." Almost every aspiring ELCA pastor I have met is afraid to check that box. Now that I live in Fargo, I know why. In the Dakotas, Lutheran churches are piled up on top of each other like Legos, but without enough pastors to match. When I asked my former student Devon why he didn't check the everywhere box, he exclaimed, "Because I'll end up living in North Dakota! And I *hate* the cold!"

I wanted to be able to judge Devon for this. But how could I, when I used to *be* him? All I can conclude now is that nothing as petty and silly as the weather should hold us back from going where we are needed most. When God calls us, we need to go. I mean, imagine if when God invited Abraham and Sarah to the promised land, they'd RSVP'ed, "Nahhh, God, we're not really into the whole desert thing. We hate the heat, so we're gonna stay put. But thanks anyway for offering to make of us a great nation!"

Remember how in an earlier chapter I said that I'd always wanted to be called Jacqueline, but people never would? Well, guess what? I finally found a place where everyone does: Fargo, North Dakota.

Every place I ever moved, I tried to start out going by Jacqueline, but in time someone would shorten it to Jacquie (usually without permission). When I moved to France to study abroad for a year in college, I thought, *This is my chance! Jacqueline's a French name, so I'm golden!* But no. Two weeks into my homestay with my French family, my French host-sister Elodie appeared in my bedroom doorway and asked, "Jacquie, tu vas manger avec nous?" I sighed and lost all hope. I mean *mon Dieu*, if you can't be called Jacqueline in France, then you don't stand a chance anywhere!

The minute I moved to Fargo and arrived on campus at Concordia College, I introduced myself to everyone as Jacqueline. And for the first time in my life, the name stuck. Sure, a few folks took the liberty of shortening it, but I corrected them tout de suite, and they listened. I was astonished at how good being called Jacqueline felt. As if I belonged. As if I was home, but home was a place I'd never been. I've never told my friends at Concordia how much I love them for this.

This may sound crazy, but becoming Jacqueline seems connected—consciously or unconsciously—to other simultaneous changes for the better in my life. In Fargo, I feel like Myself 2.0. While living here I, Jacqueline, found the courage to write the book I'd always wanted to write, *Outlaw Christian*. The book that disclosed to the whole world my authentic grief, faith, questions, and struggles. I don't think it's a coincidence that when people at last began to call me by my authentic name, I wriggled my way out of my childhood faith exoskeleton into a more mature faith.

What's more, while writing that book, I realized for the first time the deep significance of the name Jacqueline, which, as I said earlier, is the feminine version of Jacob. The biblical Jacob gets a new name after he wrestles with the angel of God down by the river Jabbok. "So he [the angel] said to him, 'What is your name?' And he said, 'Jacob.' Then the man said, 'You shall no longer be called Jacob, but Israel, for you have striven with God and with humans, and have prevailed'" (Genesis 32:27–28). Jacob thus became Israel, a name I translate as *God-wrestler*. Now, if you've read my book or known me for five seconds, then you know I'm a God-wrestler, too. The name fits me as well as an apple's own peel. And, like Jacob, once I brought my God-wrestling out into the open, I got a new name to match.

Jacob's story shows new names go hand-in-hand with new being. In my previous workplace, I made mistakes I never want to repeat, like losing my temper with a bullying colleague. I vowed that at my new job, I would do better at embodying nonviolence and compassion. I don't always succeed, but I can say I've never once in six years lost my temper with a colleague at my new institution. In many ways, the person I am now feels more like the person God dreamed of down by the river. Maybe being called Jacqueline was all the summons I needed to become her.

Maybe home is anywhere love calls you by the right name.

Remember those six-word memoirs I told you I asked my students to write? Sitting beside them, I wrote my own as well. Here it is:

Fargo has taught me: Follow your calling, for it will lead you home. Kiss fear on the forehead, and send that rascal packing. Go where you're needed—wherever that may be—and you'll find yourself saying with Jacob, "Surely the Lord is in this place—and I did not know it! . . . This is none other than the house of God, and this is the gate of heaven" (Genesis 28:16–17).

Fargo Lesson Three:
Something Good **Can** Come Out of Nazareth

I once drove my Prius from North Dakota to California. I was stopped at a red light in downtown Los Angeles when a pedestrian stopped in the crosswalk right in front of me. Shaking his head, he looked up at me, then back down at the car. He was eyeing my North Dakota license plate. It might as well have said Neptune.

One of my favorite comedians, Stephen Colbert, did an entire skit denigrating North Dakota. He joked that North Dakota was not really part of America, and that North Dakotans were foreigners "just waiting to stream into real America and take the jobs we don't want to do, like . . . living in North Dakota." I wanted to laugh but I was too ashamed, because I once stereotyped North Dakota the same way—if I ever even thought of North Dakota at all. Living in North Dakota has taught me: within myself exists a basket of biases I didn't even know about.

Unfortunately, like Colbert, many people on the East and West Coasts refer to our state as one of the *flyover states*. Coastal folks consider the Dakotas useless tundra, good only for providing the oil needed to fuel their planes to fly over that midland in order to get to each other. Of course, most Americans who hold this prejudice don't actually know anyone from North Dakota. After all, there are only 750,000 of us in the entire state.

The real problem is contempt spreads like a rash. Once we deem a place undesirable, we itch to smack that same label on the people who live there. Thus, North Dakotans—like much of rural America—are wrongly assumed to be backward country bumpkins. In many people's minds, we're kin to the folks lampooned on *Dukes of Hazard*—uncultured, poor farmers who wouldn't know the Leaning Tower of Pisa from the Empire State Building. If Fresno is sexy skinny jeans, Fargo is frumpy overalls.

What I never realized until I moved to North Dakota was how terribly wrong and hurtful this single story is. Now I recognize how deeply it scrapes the skin of the people who live here—especially the young folks. My first year teaching at Concordia, my lovely student Amanda Smith wrote this in her paper: "When I went through middle school, I felt there was nothing I could do. I was from Grand

Forks, North Dakota, the middle of nowhere. Friends would return from travels telling how people would question if North Dakota was even part of the states or a part of Canada. I didn't matter. I couldn't matter. My dreams of changing the world I kept to myself for fear of being laughed at. But being in this class has helped wake me up from society's coma and see I am not the only one who wants to change the world. . . . This entire class has been a hope meditation for me. Now . . . like Alice Walker stated [in our course reading], 'Everything I would like other people to be for me, I want to be for them.'"

Fargo, North Dakota, reminds me of Nazareth, Jesus' hometown. Nathanael, in the Gospel of John, believes that nothing good can come from that place. "Philip now went off to look for Nathanael and told him, 'We have found the Messiah!—the very person Moses and the prophets told about! His name is Jesus, the son of Joseph from Nazareth!' 'Nazareth!' exclaimed Nathanael. 'Can anything good come from there?' 'Just come and see for yourself,' Philip declared" (John 1:45–46 LB).

Nathanael's disdain indicates that people in Jesus' day believed not only that Nazareth itself was backward, isolated, and undesirable but also that everyone who was from there was as well. Biblical scholar James Metzger explains, "From what we know today about the small, rural hamlet of Nazareth, the vast majority of the townspeople were likely peasant farmers engaged in the notoriously precarious occupation of subsistence agriculture and so could conceivably be classified among 'the poor.'"[1] In other words, Jesus came from a town that most people thought of as rural and poor. Jesus' elitist contemporaries believed this made him a laughingstock rather than the Prince of Peace.

In stark contrast, the gospel insists that where you're from doesn't determine one iota of your worth or your potential. No wonder Jesus describes the gospel as good news—*to the poor*. Jesus being from Nazareth makes the powerful point that God loves those communities we view with contempt. Jesus being from Nazareth means that haters are dead wrong, about pretty much everything.

Something—or rather *someone*—good can and did come out of Nazareth. Sadly, a lot of people missed it. They were too busy making fun of his sandals.

Even today, most of us are Nathanaels. Whether it's an inner-city street or an immigrant detention center, a soup kitchen or a homeless shelter, a Flint or a Fargo, a Baghdad or a Bangkok, a prison or a methadone clinic—we still have our Nazareths. We don't go and see for ourselves. We don't get to know the people who live there. Instead, we clutch our basket of biases even closer to our chests. Meanwhile, everyone in Nazareth knows exactly what single story we tell about them.

How, then, do we live out God's call to love without limits in this day and age? We love the places—and the people—everyone else has taught us to hate. We see promise and potential where everyone else sees wasteland and wilderness. We find beauty in the badlands. We treat every Nazareth as if it were our hometown.

Fargo Lesson Four:
Survivors Love the Small Things

When I first mentioned the possible job at Concordia to my husband, he looked up from his iPad and pronounced, "I would rather die than live there." As Matt had already generously followed me to the un-sunshine state of Ohio for my first job, he had earned veto rights.

In the end, though, both Matt and I came to see this as a dream job—worth even a move to the Arctic. Once we moved, he made a vow. He would never—and I do mean *never*—complain about the weather. He didn't explain why, but I sense it was because my husband believes (1) if you're going to do something, it should never be half-assed, (2) complaining about things you can't control is a colossal waste of time, and (3) whining about winter is boring and cliché, and who wants to be either?

Impressively, Matt has kept his vow. We are six winters in, so his fortitude is astonishing. He gets up many mornings at 6:00 a.m. to snowblow for two hours so that I can get the car out of the garage. To try to make myself feel better about my own churlishness, sometimes I try to bait him into complaining. Once he's inside, peeling off his goggles and clothes frozen with sweat, I'll ask, "How is it out there?"

"Not bad!" he'll exclaim, and praise his Omni-Heat jacket, which he claims keeps him warm at all times. "No such thing as bad weather, only bad clothing!"

I sigh and feel like a loser, but the truth is, he's right. You can dress for the weather. The truth is: a positive attitude may annoy and cloy, but it also rubs off. Positivity is like patchouli. It clings to your clothes all day long, whether you want it to or not. You—and everyone around you—can't help but breathe it in.

One winter when we got sixteen inches of snow in late April, I lost my patience. "Our house is so cold!" I whined. "Why do we have to live in this forsaken place?"

My husband answered, "This place is a castle to me because I get to live in it with you." And *bam*: the scent of patchouli, everywhere.

When spring comes (the first day of the year over fifty degrees), everyone in Fargo rejoices together as if they had just completed the Ironman triathlon. (Which, in a way, they did.) It's as if God—happy toddler style—turned all the houses upside down and shook them. Everyone falls out like a liberated Fisher-Price toy, wearing bright colors and grins. Individual joy is lovely, but collective joy is downright magnificent.

My second winter in Fargo was the longest winter on record since Laura Ingalls Wilder's *The Long Winter*, which took place between 1880 and 1881. (I wish I were kidding.) The thermometer had been below freezing since October. On April 27, we finally broke fifty degrees, and I recall that April 27 as vividly as if it were epoxied to my eyelid. I was sitting in my writing room at home, looking out the window. A housefly landed on the screen. My heart leapt at the sight of its bugged-out beautiful green eyes, which I had not seen for seven months. I cried. I mean actual tears. Down my actual face.

Pathetic? Maybe. But maybe not. I mean, crying tears of joy at the sight of a fly pretty much telegraphs a newfound love for the small things. I had always considered houseflies annoying pests, never harbingers of heaven. But Fargo changed me.

I now see myself—and everyone around me—as survivors. I see everyone's spring as hard-won. Every day in this world people survive the unsurvivable, and most of the things they survive are a hundred times worse than a Fargo winter. I know for a fact this is true about my husband, and I'd bet my life it's true for tons of other people too. Genuine *love* asks us to remember this about one another, and to see other people's actions in light of what they have survived. Survivors survive because despite how long their personal winter dragged on, they rediscovered joy in the small things.

Ask any survivor and they'll tell you: when we rediscover our love for the small things, a love for the God of the small things is not far behind.

Fargo Lesson Five:
Life Is Both-And, Not Either-Or

In Fargo, everyone jokes there are four seasons: winter, more winter, even more winter, and who-the-hell-brought-the-equator-here? Although summer in Fargo lasts only about six seconds, the mercury miraculously manages to top one hundred degrees. North Dakota boasts the nation's most extreme temperature range—the coldest days on record, as well as the hottest—with annual temperature swings of up to 150 degrees. In short, Fargo is as two-faced as a double agent.

In July, when it's a hundred degrees in Fargo, I can't believe that the lush green landscape around me could ever become as cold and white and forgotten as the dark side of the moon. Likewise, in February, when not a wisp of color is in sight, the thought of a peony peeking through my back fence is preposterous. And yet, both happen in the very same yard, every year, without fail.

When my mother got sick, I fell into a depression as long, brutal, and brittle as Fargo's longest season. I never dreamed I would feel safe in the world's arms again. That peony took forever to bloom, but peek its pink face through the fence it finally did. Sometimes it's good to be wrong.

And never in my wildest dreams did I think I would be wrong about Fargo, but boy, was I. I set out to tolerate Fargo, because I felt called there. But instead here's what happened: I fell in love. Most of the time I'll deny being in love with Fargo, North Dakota, the way as a sixth grader I denied crushing on the most unpopular boy in school; or the way as an adult, I deny loving Taylor Swift songs. But denial is like those sunglasses worn by off-duty movie stars; their shallow disguise fools no one.

As a Christian, the fact that I have grown to love Fargo is a spiritual breakthrough. I prefer simplicity. I want to be able to label some people and things as *good*, others as *bad*. I like to know where I stand and what to expect. When life's either-ors start collapsing into both-ands, my mind gets muddled and I start letting the shoddy parts eclipse the stellar. Family drama keeps me awake until dawn, and I sweat worry onto my sheets. A hurtful comment from a coworker sends me into a tailspin. The injustice of the world overwhelms me, and I start to slip into despair.

Although I am loath to admit it, this is why Fargo is good for me. Life itself—the world as well as the people within it—is as mercurial as Fargo: subject to extreme mood swings; capable of both tenderness and torture; spawning both gardenias and glaciers. We can't lose sight of either pole of the planet, lest we risk becoming Pollyannas on the one hand, or hopeless cynics on the other.

In addition to unjustly allowing winter to run roughshod over the other seasons, Fargo subjects those within its embrace to wild winds, raging floods, tumultuous mood swings, and a nasty mud season. When I stop and think about it, Fargo is more like me than I'd like to admit. Yet miraculously, God and other people love me in spite of my at times insufferable personality. By loving Fargo, I'm just paying it forward.

Fargo uses the seasons to force me to feel the reality of the both-and in my very bones. I have long believed that Christians are called to acknowledge the both-and nature of life. Most people want to pretend the world's core is either-or, because life is easier if we ignore all that messy ambiguity and complexity. But real life is a paradox stew, served steaming. As G. K. Chesterton said, a paradox is just the "truth standing on her head trying to attract attention."[2]

Take, for example, these essential paradoxes, without which our faith freezes. We are all saints and sinners, simultaneously (Martin Luther). We are God's enemies, as well as God's BFFs (Romans 5:10). Jesus is both human and divine. The kingdom of God is both already and not yet. The world is both wrecked and redeemed. People are both beautiful and broken, cruel and compassionate. Life is both hellish and hopeful, sublime and shitty. Our souls are filled with angels and angst, wonder and worry. God loves both the poor and the rich, the Christian and the Muslim, the Democrat and the Republican, the gay and the straight, the member of the NRA and the member of Greenpeace.

Rather than ignore these both-ands of life, Christians should show the world how to bravely inhabit them. Radical love means courageously accepting the world—and the people in it—as they are, in all their impossible both-and splendor.

Normal is either-or. Normal is overrated. Nothing about *agape* is normal. Christians should be like Fargo, north of normal.[3]

Chapter 8

IS IT WRONG TO LOVE OURSELVES? (FEET)

Now that I, your Lord and Teacher, have washed your feet, you also should wash one another's feet. I have set you an example that you should do as I have done for you.
—John 13:14–15

How beautiful are the feet of those who bring good news!
—Romans 10:15

Last week, at a conference for pastors in our state, our bishop did something north of normal. Emulating the way Jesus expressed love for his disciples, the bishop washed the feet of all the pastors who serve under him. The pastors looked embarrassed. Their feet were grungy and misshapen, calloused and inelegant. The ugly feet reminded me of something: the parts of my mom's story that I'd rather hide from myself and from you.

Sometimes when people close to us die, we honor their memory by recalling—and sharing with others—only the best things about them. Death draws a halo around the person's head. We mean well when we do this. We assume a love without limits remembers only the good; we ask death to swallow the rest.

Here's one of the most heartbreaking confessions I've ever made: I'm guilty of this when it comes to my mother. All the things I told you earlier about her are absolutely true. But—and I'm crying as I type this—they spin a single story. Like every single story, this one's dangerous. It buries important truths—especially about self-love—beside her in the grave.

You deserve better. You deserve the whole story. So here goes; meet my mother's feet.

Feet Story #1: The Slippers

One summer, as usual, I was home from graduate school and helping care for my mom, who was sick with Alzheimer's. The evening was chilly, and I was reading a book. My bare feet stuck up in front of me on the beige leather ottoman. My mom came out of her bedroom. She looked blankly at me on the couch; she appeared to have no clue who I was. She turned around and walked straight back into her room. A few seconds later, she came back out. She carried in her right hand a pair of blue slippers. They were her favorite pair, hand knit by her favorite aunt, Pauline. Without a word, my mother walked over to me, knelt down on one knee, and slipped the slippers on my feet. As she walked away, I noticed something. Her own feet were bare.

This story about my mom's radical love for me has always been one of my favorites. But for many years I never noticed the scratch in its paint. There is one person my mother's radical love forgot: herself.

If you're like most people, when you hear this story of my mom and the slippers, you see only its beauty. As a young person, I accepted my mom's selfless slippers without question, as if, by nature of being her daughter, I somehow had a right to them. As an adult, however, I can't stop feeling unsettled by my mother's cold bare feet. What she did was stunningly beautiful, *and* (not but!) when you look at the bigger picture, beauty's not all there is to it.

Many people of faith are trained to see selflessness like my mother's as pure good. Christians—especially Christian women—are taught that self-forgetting or self-emptying is the goal of a dedicated Christian life. In the traditional Christian view of virtue, a life of selflessness flows from a loving heart like sap from a tree.

But are things always so simple? Have you ever stopped to ask yourself, is selflessness in each and every circumstance, for each and every person, always the right choice? Have you ever known and worried about someone who loved themselves too little? In my life, my mother was that person.

Hardly anyone wants to talk about it, but selflessness has its dangers. Ask any maple tree: sap holes tapped too deep can wound, and too many can kill.

Many followers of Jesus can't imagine selflessness as morally ambiguous, as having both life-giving and life-damaging potential. No doubt this is because Jesus himself was fantastically selfless. Christians therefore form in their minds a simple equation: selflessness = salvation. This is a deadly single story that omits an essential part of the tale Jesus actually told.

In Mark 12:28–31, a law professor comes to Jesus and asks him, "Which is the greatest commandment?" "The most important one," Jesus answers, "is this . . . 'Love the Lord your God with all your heart and with all your soul and with all your mind and with all your strength.' The second is this: 'Love your neighbor as yourself.' There is no commandment greater than these."

Love your neighbor as yourself. In my head, I always used to hear this commandment as slanted in one direction, the way most of us are taught. The usual interpretation: of course you already adore yourself, so now work on loving other people as much as that. But there's another way of reading Jesus' words: you already adore other people and you are fabulous at it, now remember to love yourself as much as you do them. Until I matured enough to see my mom as a whole person whose self-love had abandoned ship, this latter interpretation never occurred to me.

Surely it's possible to read the verse either way. But with devastating results, for centuries we've ignored the latter possibility. Given that Jesus spent most of his time ministering to misfits who probably believed wholeheartedly in their inferiority and inadequacy, the latter interpretation is actually super likely.

If all Jesus wanted us to do was love our neighbor, he could've made it simple and just left off the "and yourself" part. As in, *Hey, people, love your neighbors a lot.* Instead, Jesus includes love for ourselves. As in, *Hey, people, love yourself too while you're at it.*

In my view, Jesus deliberately articulated the commandment so it could be read both ways. He wanted it to offer much-needed instruction to both camps at once—those who love themselves too little, and those who love themselves too much—for certainly the world is filled with both kinds of people. Jesus wanted his words to be useful like a garden pot. Turned right-side up, a pot provides a shelter where the seedlings of self-love can take root; turned upside down, a pot cuts off the noxious weed of self-love that threatens to choke the neighbor plants.

Growing up as a faithful Christian in the deep South, I never really heard the term *self-love*. But if I had, I probably would have frowned upon it. Common live-by-the-Good-Book mantras in my household and classroom consisted of, "Don't brag," "Don't be a show-off," "Don't have a big head," "Pride goeth before the fall," "Keep your dress down," and "Women/girls are inferior to men/ boys." Okay, so the last one no one actually ever *said* in so many words, but it was pretty much scrubbed into my body with a life-lessons loofah. (Talk about self-love is important for everyone, but it's especially important for women for the reason just stated. Ditto for everyone else on earth who's been taught to view themselves as less-than.)

Centuries of male Christian teachers and preachers, however, have disparaged self-love. They see it as a deadly no-no, akin to petting a cobra. Take, for instance, one of the most popular and influential Christians teachers of all time, C. S. Lewis. In the best-selling book *Mere Christianity*, Lewis identifies pride as self-love's evil little hatchling. For Lewis, self-love and pride are the exact same thing. Both are the worst possible sins: "The real test of being in the presence of God is, that you either forget about yourself altogether or see yourself as a small, dirty object. . . . To love and admire anything outside yourself is to take one step away from utter spiritual ruin."[1] Lewis believes pride to be the source of all human misery, "According to Christian teachers, the essential vice, the utmost evil, is Pride. . . . Pride leads to every other vice: it is the complete anti-God state of mind."[2]

Lewis explicitly defines *agape*-love as the opposite of self-love. He describes *agape* as "selfless," the kind of love in which we "seek not our own."[3] In order to truly love others, Lewis argues, we must be 100 percent selfless. Think about your own experiences for a minute, and those of the people you love. Can you think of some examples where this isn't true? I sure can, and each one smashes the glass cage where Lewis holds self-love hostage.

Recently in a first-year seminar, I was teaching C. S. Lewis's chapter on pride (entitled "The Greatest Sin") from *Mere Christianity*. All my Christian students agreed: pride was the greatest spiritual sin. We discussed many of the atrocities pride has undeniably led to in the world and in our own lives. Then we switched gears. I asked the students if they could see any dangers or limitations in understanding pride to be an absolute negative. The students pondered this out-of-the-box question for a few minutes, but couldn't find an answer.

I rephrased. "Can you think of anyone for whom being told to think of themselves as a small, dirty object would be a bad idea?" One of my brilliant students, Amanda Altobell, slowly raised her hand. "Well," she said, "I suppose if someone was abused or already hated themselves or was suicidal, the last thing they'd need to hear is that to love themselves is a sin." Many years later, Amanda confided in me that she was a survivor of child abuse and abandonment who had struggled with depression and thoughts of suicide.

Amanda, age eighteen, hit upon a truth that Christian theology didn't state clearly until the 1960s, when women first started being heard as unique and valuable contributors to Christian thought. In 1960, the feminist theologian Valerie Saiving Goldstein wrote a groundbreaking essay. In it, for the first time ever, a theologian publicly disagreed with the common Christian interpretation of pride and self-love as—in all times and in all places—terrible sins.[4]

Saiving Goldstein pointed out that this point of view came largely from Christian teachers and preachers who were all powerful, well-off, and highly educated men (like C. S. Lewis). She made the case that everyone's spiritual perspective is shaped by their own lived experiences, and that these men's elite social position unintentionally biased their reading of scripture and their understanding of pride and self-love. Unfortunately, these Christian men assumed their perspective was universal, when in fact it was particular and incomplete.

Saiving Goldstein's work, along with that of others such as Susan Nelson Dunfee in the 1980s, issued a rallying cry for Christians to recognize that not everyone suffers from pride to the same degree, and some people—often women or other oppressed folks on the margins—hardly suffer from it at all. In simple terms, these brave women of faith bucked tradition and argued that some people in particular situations need more self-love, not less.

This caveat to our blanket condemnation of self-love seems obvious. But it took Christian theologians two millennia to come up with what Amanda got in three minutes. This shows how far the church and its theologians sometimes lag behind the people in the pews. If we ever want to figure out what God is up to in the world, we must respect and hear diverse voices and experiences. When those in authority refuse to listen to the beautiful, God-given voices of those who've been deemed less-than—women, teenagers, people of color, LGBTQ folks—life-saving wisdom gets lost.

Would you wear a one-size-fits-all bikini, or give one as a gift? The thought is preposterous, right? But that's all the church sold us for two millenia, when it assumed a theology written exclusively by powerful white dudes would fit everyone.

Yes, undeniably, pride has been the cause of some of humanity's most deplorable and monstrous failings. Yes, often pride and self-love are the same thing, but sometimes, they're not. Yes, some people possess way too much self-love, but other people possess barely enough to get out of bed in the morning.

For millions of people in this world, an excess of self-love is not their problem; an excess of self-loathing is. Over 3.2 million young people every year are victims of bullying. Three thousand people in the world every day commit suicide—one person every forty seconds. Millions are trapped in abusive relationships and marriages. Millions every day endure violent acts of racism, homophobia, and xenophobia. One out of four women and one out of six men, sitting next to us at church or at the coffee shop, have been raped.

Imagine how kicked in the gut it makes these children of God feel when we Christians preach *stop being so selfish; you need to love yourself less.* How could this be the gospel? I can't fathom that Jesus wants us to channel C. S. Lewis and tell trauma survivors that they're a small, dirty object. Jesus knows better than anyone that that thought already runs through so many human heads a thousand times a day, without anyone's reminding.

One more thing about my student Amanda. Amanda studied abroad with me and took five classes from me during her undergraduate career, meaning we spent over four hundred hours together. After graduation, Amanda wrote this to me in a letter: "I learned a lot from you over the last four years. But the greatest thing you ever taught me was that I was worth love."

While writing this chapter, I decided out-of-the-blue to look up the meaning of the name Amanda on-line. The search result took my breath away. The meaning of Amanda is *worthy of love.*

In my experience working with young people, I have learned that for those who feel desperately unloved, everyday conversations often bear the unseen urgency of a call to a suicide prevention hotline. More often than we realize, we are the only voice on the other end of the line, and we are called to connect God's love with those who cry out for it. One of the definitions of pride is self-respect and self-esteem. As any wounded person will tell you, these things are not always bad. On the contrary, sometimes they can save your life.

The theologian and pastor Dietrich Bonhoeffer, who lost his life for his resistance to the Nazis, once said that suffering is an "experience of incomparable value" because it teaches us to see the world "from below."[5] Today's Christian understanding of pride comes not from below, but from above. That is its weakness. The people who defined it stand at the top of the social ladder, and thus their particular temptation has always been an excess of pride, an inflated sense of their own worth as they compare themselves favorably to those at the bottom. For those who stand on the social ladder's bottom rung, however, the temptation has never been a deluge of pride; it's always been a drought.

Followers of Jesus are called to show the traumatized, marginalized, abused, and hurt people in the world the radical, liberating love of God. We start by listening to their experiences—at last. We set the cracked plate of their stories of sorrow alongside the broken cup of God's own story of pain and redemption. Next, we openly reject common Christian claims that pride and arrogance enslave everyone equally. We stop projecting our own experiences of pride, empowerment, or privilege on to those whose experience is different from ours. And finally, we redefine self-*agape* not as sin but as necessity.

Scripture supports our project of re-understanding pride from below as well as above. Notably, in the Bible, pride is primarily a position of height, "The King of heaven . . . is able to bring low those who walk in pride" (Daniel 4:37). While true that many passages denounce pride, such as, "Pride goes before destruction" (Proverbs 16:18), many also do not.

The original word in the Hebrew Bible that we most often translate into the English word pride is *ga'own*. In the Bible, *ga'own* is a good thing that only becomes ugly when human beings arrogate themselves to a position above God or one another. A more accurate translation of *ga'own*, then, as used in the negative sense, is not pride but *arrogance* (as it gets translated in Proverbs 8:13). Pride itself isn't bad, but when used as a justification to oppress other people or elevate ourselves above them, it metastasizes into evil. Simply put: the problem isn't pride, the problem is pride's excess.

Christians talk about humility as if it's a perfect good, but scripture disagrees. For example, Isaiah 49:13 declares that "the Lord has comforted his people, and will have compassion on his *anavah* ones." *Anavah* means humble; it also means "suffering" and "beaten up or beaten down." In this case, humility is not only undesirable in the eyes of God, it's something that God wants to change (contrast Proverbs 15:33).

Why does God express compassion for the humble? Because God understands that we broken human beings pervert the concept of humility to oppress, deny, bully, belittle, and keep people down and below us. *Humility* slinks to *humiliate* down a three-letter slide.

The Bible is clear: humility can be glorious, especially before God, but humility can also be dangerous, especially between sinners.

In our broken world, the Sunday School one-size-fits-all teaching of humility is dangerous because every person comes into the room desperately needing different-sized coats of self-worth to stay warm. Imagine that you have two kids, one boy and one girl. The boy is exceedingly confident and succeeds at everything. He sometimes gets a big head and acts like a bully. The other child suffers from a learning disability. She is often depressed and suffers from low self-esteem. Would you give both of these kids the exact same advice on how much they need to love themselves? Would you encourage the first child to take more pride in his actions? No? Well, neither did Jesus.

Jesus spent most of his time with the latter type of God's children—the downcast, low self-esteem folks. He knew his society taught them they were unlovable, and he dedicated his entire life on earth to unteaching this terrible lie. He wanted to convince the beaten-up and the beaten-down of this truth: *In spite of what anyone tells you, you are loved. You are a beloved child of God. Your life matters.* This irritated the heck out of the powerful people in Jesus' day who already felt loved and valued, for they tried to limit God's love to themselves. When the scribes saw that Jesus was eating with the very people they liked to humiliate, they carped, "Why does he eat with tax collectors and sinners?" And Jesus quipped back, "Those who are well have no need of a physician, but those who are sick" (Mark 2:16–17).

When Jesus commanded us to love our neighbors as we love ourselves, he spoke as a wise physician. He understood different people need different prescriptions. To the rich who believed that they already had everything, Jesus cautioned: getting into heaven will be as hard as squeezing through the eye of a needle. To the poor who felt they had nothing, Jesus lavishly promised: you will inherit the entire earth.

In the real world, the concept of humility is sadly corrupt. It's misused and abused to perpetuate humiliation or second-class status. In the past, for example, proslavery Christians used the Bible to preach humility to slaves to secure obedience to their masters, never considering the vile double standard that claiming to own another human being was the ultimate violation of humility.

Today also, the biggest problem is that our culture doesn't teach everyone to embrace their humility equally. Women and girls, in particular, are taught to embody humility much more than men and boys, which can lead to devastating differences in self-esteem and fulfillment of potential. Sheryl Sandberg's fascinating and disturbing book on gender, *Lean In*, cites an abundance of research that reveals the ways in which men in the workplace are allowed to take credit for their successes, but the same pride in women is seen as unacceptable arrogance.

When humility is considered a virtue for some and a vice for others, this is not the gospel. Instead, it's power campaigning for its own reelection. Sometimes the teaching of humility is nothing but someone else's pride in disguise. Only sin could come up with a mask so clever and convincing.

In a recent survey on domestic abuse, a shocking 60 percent of young women reported experiencing abuse from their partners and spouses.[6] One can't help but worry if these disturbing statistics have anything to do with a gross misapplication of troubling Bible verses such as "Wives, be subject to your husbands as you are to the Lord. . . . Just as the church is subject to Christ, so also wives ought to be, in everything, to their husbands" (Ephesians 5:22–24). When these same women were asked why they had not left their abusive partner, the top answer was love. Love for the person who abuses them.

If Christians define *agape* as selfless love, does that encourage women like these to leave their abusive situations or to stay in them? From the countless people of faith—both men and women—that

I've known who remain trapped in abusive relationships, I know the answer, and I'm sure you do too. It's *stay*. Love for others that completely trumps our love for ourselves sabotages lives. This is not a love without limits. It's a love with one glaring limit: ourselves.

Contrast this love of others that makes no room for love of self with Madeleine L'Engle's definition of Christian humility, which includes within itself a limitless God-given self-love. "And another lovely paradox: we can be humble only when we know we are God's children, of infinite value, and eternally loved."[7]

Feet Story #2: The Kick

One terrible day that I'll never forget I was home from college and talking to my mom in her bedroom. She leaned her salt-and-pepper hair up against the cold white wall and said, "I wish I could die. I feel like everything I do is wrong." This was not the first time she had said this, but it might well be the first time I listened.

Years later, when I started regularly seeing a grief counselor, I often found myself recounting painful stories like these. Though I always intended to talk to the counselor about my mother's illness, I often found myself talking instead about her walk-on-eggshells, always-belittled life. One day the counselor stopped me and said, "You do understand that your mom's marriage was abusive, don't you?"

No. The answer was no, I did not. I was aghast. I didn't come from an abusive family, did I? We had good times, didn't we? Didn't we have a roof over our heads? Weren't our needs met? I always thought abuse meant bruises, broken arms, and smashed furniture; not yelling, broken dreams, never letting your family visit, no ATM card, and a relentless whittling away at your self-worth. By not naming the dysfunction in my family for what it was, perhaps I hoped to pretend that it didn't exist or to avoid facing my own complicity in it. After that moment in the counselor's office, I could do so no longer.

Like I said earlier, Christians are called to call a thing what it actually is. And so I'm calling it out: *my mother was trampled upon and kicked down.* No doubt most members of my family will be furious at me for naming this, and some will scream that it's untrue. I'm angry at them for this, but I'm smart enough to see that my anger flirts with hypocrisy. How can I really blame them, when I used to *be* them?

Abusive families tell a single story about themselves: *nothing wrong here. We're all good.* To uphold my family's single story, I kept my mother's hard life a secret for nearly my entire life. But I can no longer live this lie. I can't stand by and watch a similar sadness swallow anyone else. And as a Christian, I need to muddle through with other people the messy fact that in large part, my mom's strong faith and humility made her stay, or at the very least, provided her insufficient self-worth to leave.

Would you tell a starving or anorexic person that they should eat less? Of course not. Yet this is exactly what we are doing when Christians preach to people already filled with self-loathing to scale back their self-love intake. My mom heard sermons like this all the time; I know, because I was sitting right next to her.

My friend Grayson once shared with me a haunting truth about his struggle with heroin addiction. "For so much of my life," he said, "I've wished myself gone. I don't know how else to describe it. I wish myself gone."

Many people in this world are arrogant and filled with self-adoration and pride, it's true. But we Christians need to stop preaching almost every sermon and writing every book and blog as if these were the *only* people in the world. The rest of God's children, who wish themselves gone, need a different message from the God who loves without limits.

Our theology needs to take into account that not everyone listening already loves themselves. There are people listening to us for whom pride is as foreign a concept as life on a spaceship. When we teach and preach, we can't forget people like my mother, for whom the term "self-love" sounded like Klingon. Honestly, to this day, I can't comprehend how a person who loved me so much could have loved herself so little.

I've wondered why my mother didn't leave, and I've had a heartbreaking epiphany: only someone who *believed* they deserved better could ever muster the courage to get out. And only someone who loved herself sufficiently could ever believe they deserved better. People accept only the amount of love they believe they deserve. My mother accepted a life of tiny love because she believed that is exactly what she deserved, and not a teaspoon more. Much like an anorexic starves herself because she wrongly believes she is fat, my mother deprived herself of better because the low way she was treated matched the worthlessness she (wrongly) saw in the mirror. My question assumed that my mother loved herself enough to imagine that she merited more, which of course, she did not. With all my heart, I believe that God's love without limits wanted more for my mother than for her to be walked on.

Contrary to what we might expect, a love without limits does not say to those who abuse other people, "Do anything to me that you wish, and I will stay with you." Instead, it says, "Yo. Here's the door. My self-love's too big to be in the same room with you."

Sometimes, especially in situations of abuse, we have to draw boundaries to protect ourselves from harm. I know I sound like a hypocrite here. All this talk about broadening love's bandwidth, stretching the canvas, erasing the circle, no asterisks, no exceptions, and now I'm talking about closing doors, walking out, saying no, and drawing lines in the sand? Yes, I am, and I must. A love without limits is not a rug or chair on which other people can stand or sit, it is a chandelier. A chandelier casts equal light on everyone in the room, including yourself.

Helen Beth, the same friend who taught me the left-hand writing, once attended a retreat on centering prayer, a prayer technique that uses a lot of rich, vivid visualization in order to help people heal. The retreat leader asked participants to picture in their mind's eye a person who had seriously hurt them by transgressing a personal boundary—physical, emotional, psychological, sexual—anything. "Can you see that person in your mind?" the retreat leader asked everyone present.

"Good. Now picture the boundary that they crossed. Picture it as a fence. Can you see the fence?" Everyone nodded from behind closed eyelids.

"Excellent," said the retreat leader. "Now I want you to muster your strength, and do something brave. Kick them out! That's right, you heard me. Kick them right on outta there. KICK THEM OUT back across that fence, and straight into the LOVE OF GOD."

This radical reframe has helped me and my friends practice self-love in hard situations. A few years ago I shared it with my friend Natasha, who was trapped in an abusive marriage. Natasha, a Christian and one of the most loving people I've ever known, didn't want to leave her husband even though he had physically beat her numerous times. The truth was, Natasha still loved him. Divorce, she believed, would cruelly abandon him to his addictions. She felt that to leave him would be to un-love him. In Nathasha's mind, love could never mean leaving, let alone kicking out.

But the idea of kicking someone out into the love of God helped reframe that. It set Natasha free from a false either-or. She didn't have to kick her husband out into some abyss of hate. Nor did she have to stop loving him, or stop believing that God loved him. Instead, she could live the paradox of the both-and: she could both love *and* leave. And eventually, although it was the hardest thing she'd ever done, she filed for divorce.

To *love* without limits does not mean to *live* without limits. Sometimes self-love demands we kick a person we love out of our apartment, our bed, or our life—and into the raised waiting arms of our field-goal God.

Feet Story #3: The Driving Lesson

Self-love is not universal, like blood running through our veins. Instead, it's something elusive that some people aren't born with, or that life drains out of them by suffering's daily transfusion. For still others, the harsh lash of discrimination and prejudice unjustly beats it out of their spirit. This is why so many movements for equality make positive use of the word *pride* and view that word as liberating.

Think of Black Pride during the Civil Rights movement, and Gay Pride in our day. People who have been taught not to take pride in themselves—their skin color, their culture, their personhood—must make every effort to reclaim pride in order to survive. Such pride restores dignity to those from whom it has been thieved. Such movements have nothing to do with thinking of certain people as better than anyone else, and everything to do with erasing the soul-crushing teaching that some people are less than everyone else. As long as the folks society favors refuse to see the world from below, they will never understand this.

If our society has handed you more than your fair share of pride's IT'S OKAY TO LOVE YOURSELF cards, it's time to spread the love. Self-love is like the five loaves and two fish that Jesus and the disciples used to feed the five thousand. If you're lucky enough to have been given it, its sole purpose is to strengthen you so you can feed others: "And *all* ate and were filled" (Matthew 14:21, emphasis added).

When I was touring, giving talks for my last book, a kind man in the audience in Davidson, North Carolina, said, "It inspires me that you've become a person who's able to argue with God about things you don't understand. If your mom were still around, would you have anything that you'd want to argue with her about? And are you ready to?"

The man couldn't have known it, but for decades the question, *Why, Mom? Why?* had pounded in my head in rhythm with my own pulse. However, given that my mother was already gone, I feared that no good could come in dragging that particular argument out beyond the walls of my therapist's office. I didn't want to incur the wrath of those who would hate for me for telling the truth, nor did I desire to hurt the person who hurt her. More importantly, I didn't want to hurt my mom or the beautiful way any of us remember her. I still don't want any of those things. And if the truth be told, I still love—albeit from afar—the person who mistreated her. But the man's question suggested that bringing my struggle out into the open might somehow help not only me but others, too.

I hoped he was right, but I still resisted writing this chapter. That is, until I remembered something about my mother. Strangely enough, like the slipper story, this tale was also about her feet.

When my mother first taught me how to drive, she told me to use only my right foot to both brake and press the gas. The left foot, she instructed, should never move. I obeyed. I drove only with my right foot.

A few months later, though, I was sitting in the passenger seat watching my mom drive when I noticed for the first time that she used her left foot to brake and the right to press the gas. Being a self-righteous teenager, I called her out on it. She pulled the car over to the shoulder, turned to look me straight in the eye, and declared, "I know I drive that way, but I also know it's unsafe. Don't ever copy me."

A self-negating excess of humility was my mother's left foot. She braked her whole life with it, and more than anything, she wanted to teach me not to make the same mistake. Like all the best teachers, my mother wanted her student to surpass her.

We should always be love sleuths on the lookout for what other people's lives have to teach us, even when the lesson is: *please don't ever do things the way I did.*

I've come to believe that my generous mother would want me to share with you the lessons her lack of self-love taught me, in the hopes that they might help you drive more safely. And so, with what I believe at last to be her blessing, I pass this entire chapter— and these final thoughts—along to you.

20 Things I've Learned about Self-Love

1. Self-love is a reflection of your face in the ocean of God's love for you.
2. Self-love = accepting the fact that you are God's long-lost relative.
3. Without self-love, you'll never survive this broken world. It's as necessary as oxygen for making a life sing.
4. When abusive people in this world try to hurt you, self-love serves as your only armor against them. Your self-love is God's resounding, infinite, irreversible YES to their human NO.
5. Self-love is not the same thing as self-worship, putting yourself over others, or even thinking of yourself as better than others. That is arrogance.
6. Some people in this world don't have enough self-love. They hate themselves, so they allow others to hurt them. If we Christians keep telling them that self-love's a bad thing, they'll keep on letting this happen. What's worse, we'll be the ones who made them believe they deserved it.

7. If your name is not Jesus and you give all of yourself away in love and service to others, someday you'll end up with no self left to give from. Only Jesus saves, not you.

8. Haters and oppressors and bullies will say and do anything to make you lose as much self-love as possible. They know that without it, you'll never stand up to them.

9. When it comes to the folks who want you to hate yourself, self-love is the best form of resistance *ever*. Try it and see: it drives them nuts.

10. Self-love is not always vanity; sometimes it's survival. Likewise, pride is not always arrogance, sometimes it's *agape*.

11. Everyone has their failings. For some it's pride and selfishness, for others it's self-abasement. Abasement: the word itself provides a clue as to how far down a lack of self-love wants to make you reside.

12. Though it may not be possible to love other people too much, it's definitely possible to love yourself too little. The two are not the same.

13. Self-love is something that only some people possess, like a taste for goat cheese. The good news is, like a taste for anything, self-love can be acquired, and other people can help you get acquainted.

14. "Selflessness is godliness" is healthy counsel only for people who loved themselves to begin with. For everyone else, it's toxic.

15. Think about it: Jesus says, love as God loves. And doesn't God love you just as much as God loves everyone else?

16. When Jesus told us to love our enemies, he most likely understood that for some people, that harsh label would include themselves.

17. Parts of this world are a love desert where everyone is parched. Jesus commands us not only to share the cup of God's love with others, but also to not go thirsty ourselves.

18. Jesus says: love even yourself. For many people—though we forget them as much as they forget themselves—this is what makes a love without limits so radical.

19. Self-love's only true foundation is that you are loved by a God who is Love itself.

20. The heart expands and contracts. Without either movement—inward or outward—the heart stops beating. And so God has written in our very bodies the truth of "Love your neighbor as yourself."

Chapter 9

WHY DOES LOVE HURT SO BAD?
(GRIEF)

I went about as one who laments for a mother,
bowed down and in mourning.
—Psalm 35:14

Be gracious to me, O Lord, for I am in distress; my eye
wastes away from grief, my soul and body also.
—Psalm 31:9

Our heart expands and contracts, but when we grieve, it collapses completely. For most of my adult life, Grief was my teacher. I was afraid of him and hated his classroom, but he taught me a lot about love all the same.

For many of us who've loved and lost, time spent trapped behind grief's walls hurts so bad that once our foot hits the threshold, we want only to forget and move on. I get it, but nope. I refuse. Our education costs us too much to walk away with nothing. We should at least compare notes, so here are mine.

Note #1: Love Doesn't Shame Grief

My schooling with Mr. Grief began when I was twenty years old, and in my third year of college. My mom, who was only fifty years old, started to forget stuff. I don't mean things like keys or suntan lotion. I mean things like me. One day the two of us were in the car, driving to Big Lots. A car ran a red light and almost hit us. "That was so scary!" I exclaimed, still in shock.

My mom said, "Yes, it was. But you know what's scarier? Sometimes I look at you and I don't know who is the mother and who is the daughter."

Once, on a Girl Scout trip, I saw a fish flail helplessly at the bottom of a canoe. Its mouth and gills heaved in vain to find the lost source of oxygen. When my mom forgot who I was, I became that fish.

I decided I needed to see a Christian grief counselor. When I mentioned it to my father, he reiterated the rules of my raising, "counselors are for crazy people." Somehow, grace intervened, and I ignored his advice. I made an appointment. When I arrived, the first thing I spotted was a Jesus fish over the office door—surely a good sign for a girl-turned-fish herself. I dove right in.

I confessed to the counselor that I was struggling with depression, grief, and lots of anger at God. In exchange for my honesty, she chastised, "The first thing you have to recognize is that despair is a sin against God. You know that, right? We should never grieve as one who does not have hope." My jaws gaped even wider on the canoe floor. I never went back. Not to that counselor nor to any other, for far too many side-heaving years.

I did, however, go home and look up 1 Thessalonians 4:13–14: "But we do not want you to be uninformed, brothers and sisters, about those who have died, so that you may not grieve as others do who have no hope. For since we believe that Jesus died and rose again, even so, through Jesus, God will bring with him those who have died." Read in the shadow of the counselor's interpretation, these words only compounded my grief. *Oh great,* I thought. *I'm already failing everyone around me, and now I'm failing God too.* The passage left me no comfort, only questions. Was grief a sin? A failure of faith? A sign of lost hope? Wasn't it possible to grieve and hope at the same time? What would it even look like to grieve with hope, rather than without it? Honestly, I had no clue.

In time, the seed the counselor had planted—that my grief betrayed God and that God was mad at me for it—grew monstrously large. God became to me like Snuffleupagus was to Big Bird on *Sesame Street,* except in reverse. Everyone else could see my best friend, but I began to fear that he was imaginary.

Years later, I learned that way too many of my friends and students have had similar painful grief experiences—for example, my friend Gabrielle, who was seventeen when her father died. For months it was all Gabrielle could—or wanted—to talk about. Several months after her father's death, Gabrielle was at a party at the home of a family friend. While talking about the loss of her dad with some of the guests, she started to cry. The hostess, who was in her forties and wanted her party to stay upbeat, scolded Gabrielle and said, "You know, you're not the only one who's ever lost someone." Gabrielle was stunned. She stopped talking about her dad's death with anyone until decades later. She grieved in silence. She sank into a deep depression. Gabrielle had been grief-shamed.

You've heard of fat-shaming, right? Making people feel ashamed of their bodies? Well, grief-shaming in our culture is equally a thing. We make people feel ashamed for their sadness.

Here's what we learn to do with grief in our culture: squelch it, hide it, ignore it, repress it, deny it, numb it, medicate it, forget it. And when all else fails, judge it.

In our culture, grief eats away at self-love like a flesh-eating spider. We've turned grief into one more reason for some folks of faith to hate themselves. For those whose self-love is already in low-battery mode, this added drain is deadly. Take it from me. When I was sad and depressed about my mom dying, eventually I became sad and depressed that I was sad and depressed. Things got so bad that at one point, I wished myself gone.

Think of all the clichés in our culture about pain: Don't be a Debbie Downer. Don't wear your heart on your sleeve. Don't air your dirty laundry. Don't worry; be happy. These popular sayings teach us one lesson: your grief is shameful and embarrassing—unload it as soon as you can. Since we're calling things by their right names, let's be clear: inside most of our pop-culture clichés lurks a pit viper of judgment, coiled and ready to strike.

An unhealthy number of Christians see grief as a sign of a weak and shabby faith. Many people of faith don't say this out loud like my counselor (ouch), but often you can feel them thinking it (still ouch). It's the sentiment slithering beneath sentences such as, *It's all part of God's plan*, and *She's in a better place now*. Translation: grief is a failure to trust and hope in God, a breakdown of belief in redemption and resurrection.

Jesus, however, totally disagrees. He shows us that real love grieves and lets others do the same. In John 11, Mary and Martha send word to Jesus that their brother Lazarus is sick, "Lord, he whom you love is ill." By the time Jesus gets to Bethany four days later, Lazarus is already dead:

> When Mary came where Jesus was and saw him, she knelt at his feet and said to him, "Lord, if you had been here, my brother would not have died." When Jesus saw her weeping, and the Jews who came with her also weeping, he was greatly disturbed in spirit and deeply moved. He said, "Where have you laid him?" They said to him, "Lord, come and see." Jesus began to weep. So the Jews said, "See how he loved him!" (John 11:32–36)

There are three amazing things to notice in this story.

First, Jesus, unlike us, doesn't grief-shame others. He doesn't say to Mary, "Suck it up buttercup!" Or to Martha, "Buck up, little camper, and stop mourning as one without hope!" Instead, the scriptures say Jesus feels deeply *tarasso*—literally meaning troubled or shaken up—by Mary and Martha's sorrow. Jesus responds to other people's grief with compassion, not judgment.

Second, Jesus, unlike us, doesn't say, "I'm sorry" for his tears. Instead he weeps publicly, and without apology. Jesus does this even though he resurrects Lazarus five minutes later. Jesus grieves his heart out and hopes like mad at the same time, thus proving grief and hope can and do sit side-by-side on the loveseat of your heart.

And third, the people around Jesus rightly identify the source of his grief. Not weakness, a lack of hope, or a failure to trust, but *love*. The witnesses to Jesus' tearstained cheeks cry out, "See how he loved him!" Likewise Mary and Martha observe, "Lazarus is the one whom Jesus loves!" What could God be doing here through Jesus' tears other than showing us that our grief is a legitimate response to the death of someone we loved? A love without limits cherishes every inch of ourselves and our lives, even the sad and salty stretches.

Although we feel guilt for our grief, God's limitless love enfolds and accepts it. Grief and lament are not faithlessness but faithfulness. These are valuable takeaways from John 11.

Jesus not only publicly mourns at Lazarus's tomb but also commends this practice to others: "Blessed are those who mourn, for they will be comforted" (Matthew 5:4). Jesus' own tradition, Judaism, accepts grief as a natural response to the pain of death and loss, and considers mourning an outer acknowledgment of that essential inner grief. Sixty-three times the Bible mentions that people who are in mourning dress in sackcloth and ashes. In Jesus' day, grief wasn't kept hidden or shamed; instead it was shared openly—so much so that it had its own clothes. "In that day the Lord God of hosts called to weeping and mourning, to baldness and putting on sackcloth" (Isaiah 22:12). Mourning is not maudlin, it's merely the outfit a lost love wears in public.

Throughout the Bible, the faithful—especially the prophets—grieve, lament, and mourn to express their deep love for God and God's people. Micah proclaims, "For this I will lament and wail; I will go barefoot and naked; I will make lamentation like the jackals, and mourning like the ostriches" (Micah 1:8). Jeremiah announces, "My joy is gone, grief is upon me, my heart is sick. Hark, the cry of my poor people from far and wide in the land" (Jeremiah 8:18–19). And here's how Jacob reacts to news of Joseph's death: "Then Jacob tore his clothes, put on sackcloth and mourned for his son many days. All his sons and daughters came to comfort him, but he refused to be comforted. 'No,' he said, 'I will continue to mourn until I join my son in the grave.' So his father wept for him" (Genesis 37:34–35 NIV).

The Bible records numerous moments when the faithful mourn like Jacob, by tearing their clothes. In the Jewish tradition, this tearing of the clothes—typically over the heart—is called *keriah*. The torn clothes on the outside symbolize a broken heart on the inside. Today, many faithful Jewish folks honor this biblical practice, but in more contemporary ways. At a recent conference I noticed that my friend Joshua, a rabbi, wore a small black ribbon pinned above his heart. I asked him whom he'd lost. He explained that his father had died, and that he was mourning him. I was thankful for Joshua's *keriah* pin; all of his friends were. It let us know he needed extra love, care, and space during those days.

The *keriah* fills me with holy envy. Christians today have given up the practice of wearing *keriah* due to modern-day grief-shaming. In Victorian-era Europe, however, Christian widows and mourners wore all-black mourning clothes or a simple black armband for as long as two years to signify their grief. (*Downton Abbey* aficionados:

remember when Daisy's husband died in the war, and she wore that black band on her arm for several episodes? Yeah, that.) This was the Victorian era's version of sackcloth and ashes.

What does it say about our culture and our faith today that we have no similar acceptable public signal of mourning? We know the answer. It says: *there's no room here for your grief. Your grief's too depressing, a buzzkill for our happiness.* We run our faith like a disclaimer motel: we have plenty of vacancies!* (*unless you're in mourning, then sorry, no room at the inn.)

The day after my mom died, I walked around feeling as if the sun itself had reached down and slapped me in the face while I was sleeping. I longed for a simple, acceptable, wordless way like a black armband to let others know how much I hurt. Suddenly I realized how many people's deep pain I walked around clueless to everyday, simply because it wore no color or clothes my eyes could see.

This revelation left me feeling two equally strong emotions. First, gratitude—to God, who accepts our whole selves and not just the happy-clappy parts. God not only makes room for our grief but also provides a way to help us process it—namely, mourning. God's mourning practices teach us to set aside our fear of vulnerability, so we can share our grief with one another and heal. Second, intense anger—at us. For some unfathomable reason (ego?), those of us who claim to follow Jesus choose to reject all God's wise advice. So many good people in this world today live lives of shame, secrecy, and loneliness—all because of the hidden grief lodged in the crevices of their cracked hearts. God—our God of galaxy-sized love—never intended for us to live this way.

God, in contrast to our culture, commands us to mourn and lament:

This is what the Lord Almighty says:
"Consider now! Call for the wailing women to come;
send for the most skillful of them.

Let them come quickly
and wail over us
till our eyes overflow with tears
and water streams from our eyelids.

. . . .

Teach your daughters how to wail;
teach one another a lament.
Death has climbed in through our windows."
(Jeremiah 9:17–21 NIV)

Look at the headlines today. Death has definitely climbed in our windows. Most of the time, however, we don't respond as these verses command. We don't teach one another to wail or lament. In God's opinion, lament is how the faithful give public voice to love. Unfortunately, most of us toss God's opinion in the trash as if it were a used cocktail napkin.

I've lived and taught theology in the Midwest for fourteen years now, and let me tell you: stoicism in these parts runs wild as the bison across Yellowstone. I honestly can't believe the degree to which stoicism is considered a strength, while the display of an emotion—especially sadness—is considered a weakness. My own family is originally from the Midwest, and I've only seen the men in my family cry once or twice in my entire life. My mom tried to hide her tears too, only she wasn't as good at it.

I don't understand how this absurd rule that a strong love must hide itself ever arose. More to the point, I'm baffled as to how those of us who call ourselves Christians could ever sign off on it, given that we have a savior who cried his eyes out at the sight of a dead friend and a God who commands us to lament. It's high time for a love revolution.

In my last book, I told my story of grief over losing my mom, and how in order to survive it, I turned outlaw. I defined an outlaw Christian as a person who was no longer willing to hide her grief, doubt, anger, scars, or questions from God or from other people. My students who read the book wanted to start a movement with me: *bring back the black armband!*

The God of the cross is a vulnerable God. The Latin root of the word vulnerable is *wound*. The God we meet in Jesus is a publicly wounded God, yet we insist on teaching one another to hide our wounds. We're as frightened of vulnerability as dogs are of thunder—one crack sends us cowering to the closet. Our fear knows no limits. Fortunately for us, God's love doesn't either.

In *The Smell of Rain on Dust*, indigenous author Martín Prechtel argues that all genuine grief is actually a form of praise: "Grief is praise. . . . By the event of our grief and by our wailing . . . we are also simultaneously praising with all our hearts the life we have been awarded to live, the life that gave us the . . . opportunity . . . to love deep enough to feel the loss we now grieve. . . . If we do not grieve what we miss, we are not praising what we love."[1] What a revolutionary and liberating insight!

Prechtel believes all grief must be digested and metabolized, and he makes a strong case that mourning in community is a natural way to achieve this. However, because North American culture deems most mourning unacceptable, an unhealthy portion of our grief goes unmetabolized. The result is destroyed lives and diseased families and communities.

Prechtel's words got me thinking a lot about my own troubled, broken family. Prechtel's diagnosis is spot-on—unmetabolized grief is our disease. Understanding this helped me to see certain members of my family with more compassion. And to realize families are like the sea. Their secrets are oceanic. Grief shimmers below, riotous.

Prechtel also observes that in most Native American cultures, in contrast, grief is an experience to be embraced—never repressed, feared, criticized, or judged. In Prechtel's own tradition, the person in mourning walks through the village streets shouting, wailing, crying, and beating their chest. The entire town listens and supports the grief-stricken for as long as it takes, no shushing or rushing allowed. The community considers the grieving person's cries not only healthy but necessary. They believe them to be the songs that carry the loved one's soul across the water to the other shore, where the Creator awaits.

Prechtel tells the poignant story of the time one of his white, midwestern Lutheran friends asked him for help about how best to grieve his mother's recent death. He advised his friend to cut loose: "Sing and weep with honor," Prechtel said. "Sing your mother on home."[2] The grieving friend proceeded to wail without restraint at his dead mother's funeral and graveside. The result? His relatives called him an ambulance. True story.

Our dominant Christian culture considers grief an illness—treatable only with drugs and doctors. Grief must be halted like a disease, rather than traveled through, honored, and supported by the community. *Get over it*, we tell folks. *It's time to move on.* But we've got it all backward: grief doesn't need to be healed; it *is* the healing. Grief is the blister on a cut. Not pretty, but completely necessary.

Grief doesn't need makeup or Spanx, as if it were zits or cellulite. God insists that a grieving person needs arms-open-wide, not an ambulance. We are the children of a God who is no stranger to grief, who has loved and lost as gut-wrenchingly as the rest of us. Jesus' life, as well as his death on a cross, reminds us that *God understands our grief from the inside out.* Remembering the cross means letting people talk about their crosses, no matter how uncomfortable it makes us.

But most of us don't want to go there. Certain sources of grief are even more shameful and taboo than the death of a loved one. Miscarriage, rape, abuse, addiction, discrimination, and mental illness, to name only a few. How can we ever expect folks to metabolize these losses through lament when we have not created a space where they can do so?

Someone I love very much and who is a rape survivor recently revolutionized my thoughts on this subject. I said to him, "It must be so hard for you to talk about what happened to you." He looked me straight in the eye and replied, "It's only hard if I accept the shame that other people want to put on me." Mic drop.

Note #2: Love Accepts a Scruffy Faith

My friend Barbara came to me recently in tears; she had had a miscarriage and discovered that her church didn't offer a burial or memorial service for such a loss, or even any special prayers in its prayer book. She felt forced to suffer in silence, alone, until we improvised and held our own small service in her backyard.

I often ask rooms full of Christians, When was the last time you heard a sermon or attended a vigil or prayer service at your church about miscarriage, rape, incest, or domestic violence? Most people stare at me blankly. One time a pastor posed a follow-up: Why do so many churches have a praise band, but no church has a lament band?

Church can and should be so much more than a place where we dress up, sing, talk pretty, and don a fake Barbie smile for an hour so that others will perceive us as faithful, rather than what we actually are—a struggling people with a scruffy faith. Church should be less like a palace and more like a dog park: a place where the truth bounds wildly about, off the leash at last.

I recently discovered the nifty notion of scruffy hospitality on a popular blog.[3] Scruffy hospitality means go ahead and invite people over even when you haven't vacuumed in two weeks, have nothing to eat except stale Cheetos, and the kids' toys cover the living-room floor. In other words, love cares only about authenticity, not making a good impression.

Theologians like me don't often admit this, but wow, my faith is so scruffy! Most days I'm plagued with questions I can't answer

(Why so much suffering?), anger at God I can't hide (Why don't you just show up already?), laments I can't let go (How long, Lord, how long?), doubts I can't wrestle to the ground (Does forgiveness make me a doormat?), and grief that kicks me in the gut (I miss her so much God, everyday). If faith is a coloring book, I'm definitely the kid who colors outside the lines.

I know I'm not alone in my scruffy faith. Still, Christians often insist that both our own faith and that of others be perfect. We demand faith be free of fleas, muddy paws, drool, and dingleberries. We demand it subscribe to a specific set of beliefs— namely, those of our own church or clan. People with a scruffy or messy faith get misunderstood, outlawed, mocked, shamed, and looked down upon as mutts who are not as good as the purebreds.

In the Gospel of Matthew, a scruffy faith encounters Jesus' radical love. A Canaanite woman comes to Jesus and cries out, "Lord, Son of David, have mercy on me! My daughter is demon-possessed and suffering terribly" (15:22). At first, Jesus won't even speak to her. The disciples tell Jesus to send the woman away, but Jesus refuses, and this exchange happens:

> He [Jesus] answered, "I was sent only to the lost sheep of Israel."
>
> The woman came and knelt before him. "Lord, help me!" she said.
>
> He replied, "It is not right to take the children's bread and toss it to the dogs."
>
> "Yes it is, Lord," she said. "Even the dogs eat the crumbs that fall from their master's table."
>
> Then Jesus said to her, "Woman, you have great faith! Your request is granted." And her daughter was healed at that moment. (Matthew 15:24–28)

The woman in this tale has two strikes against her. First, she's female. In Jesus' day, a single story was told about women. They were second-class citizens, on par with slaves and children. Second, she's a Canaanite—a people the Israelites considered to be idol worshippers, practitioners of a false faith. Members of Jesus' clan label her a dog, and stereotype her as less-than-human. They call people like her *heathen* and *pagan*. The disciples think of this woman's faith, along with her gender and ethnicity, as scruffy—on steroids. They assume her inferior status means that she and her Canaanite relatives shouldn't be allowed in the door of God's tent of love. In their minds, the tent is marked: "NO DOGS. Lost sheep of Israel *only.*"

At first, Jesus appears to go along with this single-story way of thinking. But the woman's response outfoxes the stereotype of her. Her words indict love's failure, call it out on the table: "You Israelites claim we Canaanites are inhuman, that we're dogs, but look: you treat your dogs way better than you treat us." It's hard to say exactly why Jesus' attitude toward the woman changes once she points out that even dogs get fed. She doesn't convert to Jesus' religion, and she doesn't seem to change one iota (she acknowledged Jesus as Lord the minute she met him, and Jesus ignored her even then).

Does Jesus misjudge the woman? Does Jesus change his mind? It sure seems like it. In this story, I believe Jesus models for us the moral courage it takes to admit when we've been suckered into buying a stereotype. And to allow ourselves to be schooled by the very person our culture insisted was too foolish to have anything to teach us.

Two more things to notice. First, something in the woman's words tugs at Jesus' heart, and Jesus acknowledges that his culture's single-story stereotype about the Canaanites fails to live up to God's no-exceptions love. And second, Jesus' love is so radical and limitless, it withholds *nothing* even from a person who does not worship the same God as he does. With the disciples as witnesses, Jesus shows love and kindness to a person his culture condemns as a second-class heathen. Or, to use names some Christians might call her by today, an *unbeliever* or *non-Christian.*

If it makes us bristle to learn that Jesus refuses to exclude these folks from God's radical love and our acts of kindness, then we've heard the story rightly. Jesus tells each of his parables in order to shock us into seeing anew the Himalayan hugeness of God's love. For some, its sheer size is awesome. For others, it's scandalous. Jesus knew it would be that way, which is why he warned, "And blessed is anyone who takes no offense at me" (Matthew 11:6).

I've never been to the Himalayas, nor did I grow up around mountains, but my first evening living in the south of Japan, I watched the sun set behind Mount Tenzan. When darkness fell, I could no longer tell where Mount Tenzan began and the sky ended. My heart started pounding. I couldn't see the mountain, but I felt it everywhere—a massive, extraordinary presence. I've never before admitted it to anyone, but I was terrified. For me, Mount Tenzan = God's love. Ginormous things with no discernible edges scare the pants off us at first. It's no coincidence that one of the Bible's names for God is El-Shaddai, which means *God of the mountain.*

Why then do we continue to exclude those with a scruffy or imperfect or even nonexistent faith from our circle of love? Perhaps our perfectionism stems from the line in the beatitudes where Jesus instructs, "Be perfect, therefore, as your heavenly Father is perfect" (Matthew 5:48). For some people, this verse makes the needle on their self-love gauge plunge even deeper below "E."

I don't believe that Jesus, who instructed us to forgive people "seventy times seven" times, demands such perfection. The Bible overflows with imperfect people whom God nonetheless chooses for extraordinary ends. David, who was a murderer and an adulterer, becomes king of Israel; Paul, who persecuted Christians, becomes the apostle to the gentiles; Peter, who betrayed Jesus three times, becomes the cornerstone of the church. Heck, God chose Mary and Joseph to be parents to the Christ child, and they lost track of him for three days (Luke 2:41–46)! These people are a far cry from perfect; so what's up?

The Greek word Jesus uses in Matthew 5:48 is *teleois*. It's the adjective form of *telos*, which is a Greek word meaning to set out for a goal, to have an ultimate goal or end. To be *teleois*, therefore, means to have a purpose, to be complete, whole, mature, full-grown. A child is *teleois*, for example, when she becomes an adult. English has no direct equivalent for *teleois*, so we often mistakenly translate it as "perfect." But honestly, it's not what Jesus meant.

Here's the entire context of Jesus' words:

> You have heard that it was said, "You shall love your neighbor and hate your enemy." But I say to you, Love your enemies and pray for those who persecute you, so that you may be children of your Father in heaven. . . . For if you love those who love you, what reward do you have? Do not even the tax collectors do the same? And if you greet only your brothers and sisters, what more are you doing than others? Do not even the Gentiles do the same? Be perfect, therefore, as your heavenly Father is perfect. (Matthew 5:43–48)

In these verses, Jesus asks us to be mature, whole, and complete children of God. To strive to fulfill our purpose, the purpose God intends for our lives. Jesus demands purpose, not perfection. Jesus wants our life to share the same goal as God's own life—love. A scandal-causing, boundary-busting, eye-popping love without limits. A love with branches so broad it shades even our enemies. The best way to say it: *God wants our love to grow up.*

If mature love creates a space for grief, lament, and scruffy faith, then our churches must do the same. One place to start is holidays and worship. Think about our customary greetings: Happy Mother's

Day! Happy New Year! These greetings may seem insignificant, but they send a strong message: *happy* is the only appropriate emotion for people of faith. Not true. Real love understands that *both* grief and joy lease the same studio apartment—your heart.

Ask anyone who's lost a child: Christmas is the worst. Or ask a motherless child like me—Mother's Day is 24 hellish hours of a thousand contradictory emotions, all stampeding through your heart at once like Black Friday shoppers. The few times I've dared mention that Mother's Day really drags me down, some folks asked, "But aren't you so grateful to have had such a wonderful mother?" Of course I am! But that's the single story again, vying for the win. Sometimes both-and is simply the truth about life. Some days are diamonds, while others are dust.

I long for our worship life to capture life's scruffy both-ands. It is possible, as I discovered last year when I was invited to attend a beautiful Mother's Day service at the Unitarian Universalist Church of Fargo. Man, those amazing folks know how to carve out space for grief and all things scruffy. During a special time of the service, members of the congregation were invited to come up, light a candle, and say out loud a joy or a grief that they were experiencing. Loss was allowed, and love was, too. The worship leader read prayers aloud that mentioned mothers who had lost children, children who had lost mothers, miscarriages, infertility, abortions, and even people who were estranged or angry with their mothers. Men and women sobbed openly.

I couldn't believe the raw authenticity I witnessed. I felt awe, like I could actually hear Love scoot her tush over on the pews and make room for everyone's whole person—warts, acne, scabs, soaked Kleenex, stretchmarks, and all. Like when we opened the door a crack to let grief in, joy slipped in too, riding piggyback.

I usually dreaded Mother's Day, all the mother/daughter teas and Hallmark happiness hoisted upon my shoulders. But on that day and at that service, I finally belonged. And the best part was, everyone else did too.

Here's another way to make room: when I was in Ohio giving a talk about my scruffy, outlaw faith, a bunch of awesome Lutherans informed me about their Blue Christmas service. Blue Christmas— yes, it's actually a thing!—is a special service at Christmastime for those who are mourning the loss of a loved one. It acknowledges the sadness, fear, and longing that surrounds the holiday for so many people.[4]

This Christmas, for the first time, I was invited to preach at a Blue Christmas service. As it turned out, my mother-in-law died just a few days prior. The service was healing for both my husband and me in way that no regular Christmas service ever could have been.

To truly love our neighbors as ourselves, we need to incorporate grief into the life of faith. Grown-up love accepts a scruffy faith. Grief is the pinch from the dream of death that can wake us up to life.

Note #3: Grief Proves that Love Outwits Death

As I sit writing this, a peach sits on the table in front of me. I pick it up and look at its fleshy face in my hand. I think of my mom and the times we went peach-picking in the Georgia orchards. I want to take a bite, but I hesitate. Although I adore peaches, it's hard for me to eat them anymore. They drip disappointment all over the place. I worry, will it be this way forever? Will anything ever just be itself again? Grief does that to you—things that were once pure sweet acquire a sour aftertaste.

T. S. Eliot in the poem "The Love Song of J. Alfred Prufrock" ponders, "Do I dare to eat a peach?" In college my professor Tony Abbott asked my whole class what the poet meant by that sentence.

I'd never before raised my hand in his class, but I blurted out, "He's asking himself whether it's worth it to make yourself vulnerable, to open up to being hurt by love."

At age eighteen, I didn't know much, but I did know why love is a dare so many won't accept. Love is delicious, but at its center awaits a hard pit. If you bite, you risk cutting your teeth on loss.

All grief is love, and all love will someday cause you grief. Knowing this, grief tries to tempt us to never be so foolish as to love again. Granted, love is a seesaw. But I choose to hike up my skirt and climb aboard anyway, even if it's unladylike, because reserve is for the dead, while soaring and splinters are for the living.

I know that grief feels exactly like love has left you, but don't let this lie fool you. This lesson took the longest for me to learn, but it just might be the most important one of all. Grief, though it's the worst thing we can go through in life, has a secret upshot—and here it is.

Grief proves that *love outwits death*. Every tear we shed over those who die is salty evidence that our love didn't disappear with them into the dirt. Instead, love lives on. If this were *not* true, grief wouldn't exist. Death would simply crush all our feelings of loss and longing and missing; we'd forget and feel no pain. In the real world, death tries its hardest to murder love. But grief exposes death as a liar, as well as a failed assassin.

My student once showed me a photo she took of a sign painted in Ferguson, Missouri, after the death of Michael Brown. It said:

THEY TRIED TO BURY US.
THEY DIDN'T REALIZE WE WERE SEEDS.[5]

Death always tries to bury love, but death is a fool. Love is a seed. Grief is its blossom.

I used to think of grief as form of hopelessness, but not anymore. Now I know: grief is the heavy feeling you get when the love that you feared had left you comes back and rests its head on your chest. When you grieve and everything in the whole aching world transforms from itself into loss, hope is actually speaking to you. *It hurts, I know,* she says. *But you know why? Because love outlasts death.* "Where, O death, is your victory? Where, O death, is your sting?" (1 Corinthians 15:55).

Love is the room where God banishes time to grieve its own death. Love lives on beyond time, and this is what Christians really mean when they talk about *eternity.*

When my student Marta's grandmother, Phyllis, was diagnosed with Alzheimer's, Marta's grandpa Bill took her to the doctor's office for tests. By then, Phyllis couldn't read or express herself very well; most days, she couldn't even remember her own name. The doctor set a pen and blank sheet of paper in front of her. "Write a sentence on the paper," the doctor instructed her, "Any sentence you can think of." Phyllis thought about it for a second and then wrote, "I love Bill."

Grief is eye-stinging, gut-wrenching, fist-clenching evidence that love speaks last. In the war against loss, grief is love's revenge. Grief is how our heart stuns us into remembering what we otherwise forget, which is: against all odds, love wins.

A student who was hurting once asked me the question "What is grief? Why do we have to go through it?" This is the parable I wrote for her, and also for you.

Imagine: in the middle of the night, a thief named Death sneaks into your house and robs your safe, stealing everything you most treasure. You rage, gnash your teeth, and file police reports. Several months pass. The police call you in, then give you the bad news: none of your valuables will ever be recovered. You walk home from the station, desolate and inconsolable. Exhausted, you enter your room, and lie down on the bed.

And that's when you see it: your most cherished possession. The antique ring that your mother gave you—the one she inherited from her mother before her and her mother before her—a ring so old no one even remembers who wore it first. You can't believe your eyes. The ring lies underneath your dresser, where the thief must have dropped it. Of all the things taken from the safe, this loss had beaten you up the most. You had planned on giving the ring away next month, when you asked your favorite person in the whole world to spend the rest of their life with you. You thought the ring was gone forever, but now you know the truth. It was there the whole time. It never left your bedside.

That's what grief is: the ring the thief forgot.

Those who grieve, proclaim the good news. Against all thieves, love survives.

Chapter 10

HOW DO I LOVE YOU IF I DON'T EVEN LIKE YOU? (DIFFERENCE)

*Those who say, "I love God" and hate their
brothers or sisters are liars.*

—1 John 4:20

*Love your enemies, do good, and lend,
expecting nothing in return.*

—Luke 6:35

Difference is one of life's most valuable teachers, but tragically, we treat it more like a thief. Like Picasso with a palette of hate, we stain the world's canvas with prejudice, stereotypes, and discrimination, using every difference between us as our paint. Political party. Passport. Faith. Skin color. Sexuality. Gender. Ethnicity. Education. Tax bracket. ZIP code. Social status. A lot of these differences—like skin color—were created by God and should be celebrated. Other differences—like the chasmic income gap between the rich and the poor—were created by us and should not only be grieved but changed. Sadly, we usually get

167

them backward or can't tell them apart. We twist even the beautiful into the broken. Instead of bridges, we build bombs. Instead of welcomes, we build walls. Where's the love broad enough, we wonder, to reach across the ravine and grab hold of people's hands on the other side?

The fallout from the 2016 election was so epic that people who used to be friends no longer even speak to one another. Many of us can't bear to go on social media anymore for fear of melting into a puddle of tears at the rage, cruelty, name-calling, and insults. Hope feels like it's eroding as fast as the Mississippi Delta.

I often ask my students to share a time when they learned something from someone else, and then tell why they were able to learn it. The stories they tell are beautiful. About a coach who cared enough to show them how to slice the ball just right, or a mom who taught them how to tie their shoes by singing the bunny ears poem. No one ever says, *I learned it because someone punched me, used profanity, screamed at me, or tweeted over and over at me that I was the stupidest person alive.* Yet somehow, we still think these are the best ways to change people's minds and fix what divides us. *Yeah,* God must be thinking, *good luck with that.*

There's an old Jewish story about a rabbi and his disciple. The rabbi, who was well-known for his piety and compassion, was unexpectedly confronted one day by one of his devoted young disciples in their house of prayer. In a burst of feeling, the disciple exclaimed, "My master, I love you!"

The ancient teacher slowly looked up from his books and then asked his fervent disciple, "Do you know what hurts me, my son?"

The young man was baffled. Composing himself, he stuttered, "I don't understand your question, rabbi. I'm trying to tell you how much you mean to me and you're confusing me with irrelevant questions."

"My question to you is not at all strange or irrelevant," the rabbi stated. "It is the very soul of understanding love and compassion. For if you do not know what hurts me, how can you truly love me?"[1]

We can't love God unless we know what hurts God. And then we need to stop doing it. Yet do we ask, or even care, how we are breaking God's heart? These days, what could hurt God more than the wounding ways we treat those who are different from ourselves?

Enemy Labeling

One way we hurt God is by calling and treating each other as enemies—as people beyond reconciliation's and redemption's reach. Jesus understood that we use the label *enemy* to designate not only those who hate us or harm us but also those *we* want to feel justified hating or harming. To get us to stop, he pleaded, "But I say to you that listen, Love your enemies, do good to those who hate you, bless those who curse you, pray for those who abuse you. . . . Do to others as you would have them do to you. If you love those who love you, what credit is that to you?" (Luke 6:27–32).

Jesus' own society—the Roman Empire—labeled him public enemy number one and condemned him to die on a cross. If the cross teaches us anything, it should be this: we are often dreadfully wrong about who we imagine our enemies to be.

Why did the powerful Romans crucify Jesus? Hate. Greed. Cruelty. Jealousy. Anger. But perhaps most of all, *fear*—fear of the scandalous love Jesus lived and taught, a love so wide and wild, deep and disorderly, it struck terror in the hearts of all those who normally wielded the power to decide who was loveable and who was not.

Today's psychologists have a name for how people at the top often react to times of revolution or upheaval: *elite panic*. This term perfectly describes many people's response to Jesus' radical love revolution. Every time Jesus loved the unlovable, held a leper's hand, or shared hummus with outcasts, the elites freaked out. They (rightly) felt their power slipping away from them—the power to designate who was stranger or friend, heathen or believer, prophet or sinner, whore or king.

Jesus not only challenged the people's imperious power to label one another the salt or the scum of the earth, he declared the labels themselves meaningless. And so, the people did to Jesus what we still do today to people we don't understand or feel threatened by—they labeled him a criminal, and they killed him.

Jesus led with love, while many of his contemporaries led with labels. Today, we are no different. One can only hope that someday, we will be as Easter-dumbfounded as they must have been to discover that love lives on, in spite of our best attempts to crucify it.

Pondering the cross makes me imagine the kingdom of heaven like this.

Once upon a time the world had one queen. She loved her people more than anything, but was bone-tired of their constant bickering and refusal to share. With a wave of her scepter, she eliminated every label, brand, and logo from the world. From every tennis shoe, sweatshirt, and box of baby wipes to every map, bank sign, and can of soup—not a single label remained. Utter corporate chaos ensued. The Dow Jones plummeted to zero. The corporations vowed to assassinate the queen. Many people despaired. But others celebrated, and danced in the streets.

That's what the kingdom of heaven will look like—a label-less universe. Jesus asks us, *will you be the person who panics, or the one who parties in the promenade?*

As I shared at the start of chapter 6, an enemy is a person whose story you haven't yet heard. In my life, I've had far too many painful reminders of this lesson. But one in particular stands out.

A few summers ago, my husband and I spent several weeks at a Christian family summer camp in the North Carolina mountains. The families hiked, rode horses, prayed, and shared meals together. It was beautiful, relaxing, and perfect. Or at least it would've been, if it hadn't been for *them*, the Battsons.

The Battsons were a family at camp who bounced up and down on my last nerve. The parents, Justine and Jared, had two small children—Annie and Maddy, ages four and five. Annie and Maddy were terrors. During every meal, they ran about the room like cougar cubs on cocaine. They yowled, scratched, clawed, and head-butted into your knees as you tried to deliver your tray to the kitchen. They never ate, and looked unhealthy and thin as rails. Justine and Jared did next to nothing to rein them in—not even ask them to sit down!

The worst was the evening worship service, which we held in the woods. Many of us—myself included—looked forward each day to the beauty and tranquility of that quieting-down hour. But almost every night, it felt ruined. We could barely hear the hymns over Annie's and Maddy's shouts, cries, and pounding footsteps. *Truly,* some of the other campers and I complained behind their backs, *We've never seen anything like it. They act more like two-year-olds! Why don't their parents do something?*

We were a few days away from camp's end when Justine struck up a conversation with me about the study I'd just led. I'd made a comment about how much you never really know about what's going on in other people's lives, but that God knows. Justine said, *Yes, well that's just like Annie and Maddy. Let me tell you their story.* And this is what she said.

Jared and Justine adopted Annie and Maddy, who were biological sisters, when they were two and three. Their bio-parents were drug addicts who lived in and out of various motels across the Carolinas. The bio-parents enjoyed partying without being dragged down by childcare, so they'd often leave Annie and Maddy alone in the motel rooms. Before they'd leave, they'd strap Annie and Maddy into their car seats, put a bottle or two in their little laps, and leave them there for two, maybe three days at a time. Annie and Maddy managed to feed themselves, but Annie, being younger, couldn't burp in the leaning-back car seat. So Annie, to relieve her own gas, taught herself to throw up every time she ate. Today, the kids still can't stand to be in a car seat or high chair or really, a seat of any kind, and Annie struggles with childhood bulimia—instinctively vomiting every time she eats. "It's so hard to keep any weight on her," Justine concluded her story, "But we're doing the best we can."

If a person could drown in her own shame, I'd be dead.

Listening to Justine made me feel like I'd stepped into one of Flannery O'Connor's short stories, wherein grace always happens through violence, robbery, drowning, or getting shot. I thought about her bizarre story *Revelation*, in which a girl named Grace knocks out a self-righteous woman named Ruby by throwing a huge book at her head. I never understood that story until Justine showed me its meaning. Ruby = me. The book = Justine's story. Grace = Herself. Like anything that makes you stay woke, grace hurts.

My neighbor Sarah recently told me a story about giving birth to her daughter, Perry, at the local hospital where her husband works as a surgeon. Once Perry was born and Sarah was resting, a nurse came by to fill out Perry's official birth certificate. "Father's name?" the nurse asked. Sarah stated her husband's full name (the nurse no doubt had heard of him since they worked at the same hospital). "Mother's name?" Sarah clearly spelled out her full name, including her last name, which was different than her husband's. To Sarah's surprise, the nurse snorted with contempt and made a disparaging comment about women who keep their maiden name. She then asked what last name the baby would have (her dad's), and Sarah spelled out Perry's full name. Sarah was a little put-off by the nurse's judgmental attitude, but quickly forgot about it in all of her joy at the new baby.

That is, until a few weeks later, when Perry's birth certificate arrived in the mail. Sarah opened it, and was shocked. On the line next to MOTHER'S NAME, it said: SARAH UNKNOWN. The passive-aggressive nurse had found a way to express her discontent. Of course, the nurse had known Sarah's real name—not only had she told her, it was correct on her wristband as well as every hospital bill and insurance form. Even though Sarah laughed and joked that I should put this story in my next book (and she'll laugh even harder when she sees I actually did), deep down, she was hurt.

Have you ever been treated as an unknown? It hurts terribly, doesn't it? Everyone longs to be known more than they are now—by other people, God, and even themselves. But sadly, even though we don't want to be treated as if our name were UNKNOWN, we continue to treat certain people as if that were theirs. Sometimes this is because we don't like their choices, beliefs, behavior, skin color, sexuality, or politics. Sometimes it's because we've written that person off as too different, or as an enemy, or simply not worth the time to get to know. But no matter our excuse, what we're really doing is robbing people of their humanity.

To label anyone an enemy is to do what the nurse did—take a living, breathing child of God and turn them into an unknown. This crushes not only that person's heart, but God's. God's love refuses to label anyone unknown: "Before I formed you in the womb I knew you, before you were born I set you apart" (Jeremiah 1:5). The Psalmist declares, "O Lord, you have searched me and known me. You know when I sit down and when I rise up; You . . . are acquainted with all my ways" (Psalm 139:1–3).

What hate labels *unknown*, love labels *known*. In fact, according to scripture, to love *is* to know: "For now we see only a reflection as in a mirror; then we shall see face to face. Now I know in part; then I shall know fully, even as I am fully known. And now these three remain: faith, hope and love. But the greatest of these is love" (1 Corinthians 13:12–13).

In the kingdom of love without limits, no enemies reside.

The "Less-Than" Label

A second way we wound God is our insistence on labeling some folks "less-than." Such folks are not only inferior, we claim, but also "dangerous"—people we need to stay away from. We use fear to create exceptions, as well as reasons to exclude certain people from our love, care, and kindness. And eventually, to exclude them from having equal access to things like health care, clean water, education, or food. The less-than label breeds injustice as fast as a manure farm does flies, and with the same stink.

To love God is to stop making exceptions. "What does the Lord require of you but to do justice, and to love kindness, and to walk humbly with your God?" (Micah 6:8) It's clear what God calls people of faith to do, so why aren't we doing it?

I should begin with the question, *Why aren't I doing it?* The answer is simple: *I am afraid.* Consider Jesus' summons to become good Samaritans. Although I wouldn't hesitate to stop and help someone I knew and loved, I make an exception for helping unknown people, especially men I don't know. My fear isn't irrational, especially as a woman. Many of us have suffered harm at the hands of strangers, or know someone who has. The crime show *Forensic Files* is full of stories about caring people who stopped to help but ended up dead in a ditch.

My Christian ethics students often ask me questions like: How much self-protection and stranger danger is okay, and how much is too much? Does God want us to risk being hurt, raped, or killed in order to help someone else? In such a violent world, how do we become good Samaritans? *How far does God really expect our love to go?* I always admit that I too wrestle with these same questions.

Then, I tell them a couple stories—both of which have made me see that for as many times as my fear is perhaps justified, more likely it's an excuse for my apathy and prejudice.

In 2009, my students and I went to Khayelitsha, South Africa for a month to learn about the unjust legacy of apartheid. We stayed with families who taught us that the township of Khayelitsha exists because of racism. During apartheid, a government-sanctioned era of segregation, the white supremacists in power made it illegal for black South Africans to remain in the cities. The whites stole black people's homes and livelihoods, forced them to relocate to segregated townships like Khayelitsha, and refused to pay for any infrastructure.

Even though apartheid officially ended in 1994, the effects of this injustice still linger. In 2009 when I visited, Khayelitsha was 99 percent black and remained one of the most impoverished townships in the nation. Many of the homes and shacks didn't have a roof, electricity, or indoor plumbing. Most of the streets lacked signs, streetlights, or pavement. My host family's house didn't have an official postal address because, they said, many of the township neighborhoods remained unmapped, even after thirty-five years.

One day during our stay in Khayelitsha, my student Emily and I accidentally got off at the wrong bus stop on our way home. The unmarked roads were a dusty maze. We had no cell phone or map. In minutes, we were hopelessly lost. Dusk descended. My heart rate ascended. As we paced up and down the same street for the third time, two black South African women stopped to help. The only white people on the street, we stood out like a sore thumb.

"Sisters," they addressed us. "Are you lost?"

"Oh my, yes!" We cried out with relief. "Can you please help us?"

We told them the name of the family we were staying with. They nodded their heads. We were in luck. They knew where they lived. The two women promptly dropped their own plans and safely escorted us home—a thirty-minute walk. When we got to our house, they hugged us goodbye and then risked their own safety, by walking back home in the dark.

Later that night, Emily and I marveled at the outrageous kindness of the two women, who had legitimate reason not only to fear us but also to despise us. After all, people with skin our color had oppressed them their entire lives.

Growing up as a white kid in the southern United States, I was taught a single story about people with black skin. "They" were "not like us"; they were strangers to fear and avoid. In contrast, black women in South Africa called me sister.

I thought of these women years later when one day in Fargo, my husband and I were walking home together from the gym. Outside the YMCA, I spotted a Native American young man—late teens or early twenties—standing at the side of the road. I don't know why he caught my attention, but he did. All the other passersby kept a safe distance, as I probably would've if Matt hadn't been with me. The young man was pacing and talking to himself and wiping his eyes as he stood next to a pedestrian walkway. A lot of terrible, arguably racist things that I'm ashamed to admit ran through my mind like, "I don't have time to get involved here," and "What if he asks me for money?" and "What if he has a mental illness and hurts me?" But the distress of the young man hummed in the air like a high-voltage power line, so loud it drowned out these selfish thoughts. Remembering my South African sisters, I approached.

"Are you okay?" I asked the young man.

"No," he sniffed, visibly shaken. "I was hit by a car three months ago at this intersection. The car hit me and never even stopped." He lifted up his shirt to show terrible bruises on his torso. "I'm too scared to cross the road," he said, looking down at his feet while shame colored his face ear to ear. Little did he know how much his words filled me with a shame of my own.

"That's awful," I said. "I'm so sorry that happened to you. Do you want me and my husband to walk with you? Maybe if we stand on either side of you, you'll be able to make it across."

He thought about this for a few slow seconds, then mumbled, "Okay."

Like bodyguards, Matt and I flanked him, each touching an elbow. "You can do it," Matt said softly. The young man trembled as he stepped off the curb. He walked with a slight limp and feverish glances to the right and left.

"You've got this," I encouraged him. We made it safely to the other side. The young man stepped up on the sidewalk, thanked us, and walked on his way, straightening his blue backpack.

To this day, when faced with similar decisions, I try not to do what I usually do, which is keep walking. I try to remember my brother and how all he needed was someone alongside him as he crossed the street. That memory whispers in my ear: *Sometimes Love picks the lock to your heart and takes over the space Fear used to rent. Please, please, please don't evict her.*

This memory also reminds me: kindness doesn't make me anyone's "savior." Only Jesus is a savior; we are merely wannabe Samaritans. As Shane Claiborne once said while speaking on my campus, *I'm not Jesus; I'm just the ass he rode in on.*[2]

In Davidson, North Carolina, the town where I went to college, there's a statue of a homeless Jesus. He lies on a park bench, covered in a blanket. Nail holes mark his uncovered feet. He lies in front of a church in a well-off neighborhood. The sculptor, Timothy Schmalz, says the piece represents Matthew 25:42–45, "For I was hungry and you gave me no food, I was thirsty and you gave me nothing to drink, I was a stranger and you did not welcome me, naked and you did not give me clothing, sick and in prison and you did not visit me. . . . Truly I tell you, just as you did not do it to one of the least of these, you did not do it to me."

When the statue first appeared, a woman who lived nearby thought it was a real person and called the cops. Other neighbors complained that homeless Jesus demeaned the neighborhood.[3] Several other cities acquired their own homeless Jesus statues, but London banned homeless Jesus saying he "would fail to maintain or improve the character or appearance of the Westminster Abbey."[4] Westminster Abbey, of course, is a church. Shakespeare himself couldn't have penned such irony.

Jesus was homeless. Jesus was also poor, a lawbreaker, a death row inmate, a refugee (Matthew 2:13–14), and a man of Middle Eastern descent. When Mary Magdalene came to the tomb on Easter morning, she mistook the resurrected Jesus for the gardener. Today, we would mistake him for a terrorist. Or a freeloader, or a guy looking for a handout, or one more of "those people" who are trying to take away the jobs of hardworking Americans. Given the labels we'd for sure smack on Jesus, one thing is certain: if we didn't outright hate him, we'd at the very least consider ourselves vastly superior to him.

If the Bible is any indication of God's priorities, nothing hurts God more than the way we treat the poor, whom the Bible mentions over two thousand times. "Is not this the fast that I choose: to loose the bonds of injustice, to undo the thongs of the yoke, to let the oppressed go free, and to break every yoke? Is it not to share your bread with the hungry, and bring the homeless poor into your house?" (Isaiah 58:6–7). Yet, how do we treat those who live in poverty? Most of us Christians wouldn't dream of bringing the homeless poor into our houses; but we wouldn't hesitate to call the cops on them.

Sin is not only individual, it's infrastructural. It's more than just something I do; it's also something *we* do. We-sin is harder to spot, a snake in the grass. No one person is to blame for racism, sexism, ableism, classism, ageism, homophobia, Islamophobia, and all the rest, but that doesn't make those things any less real or their fangs any less sharp. Until we admit these -isms, our love has limits, because we're ignoring the real, wet, salty tears of those who are hurt by them.

Jesus once got so livid about how badly the rich were exploiting the poor, he overturned the tables in the temple (Matthew 21:12–13). He then quoted Jeremiah 7:11 (NLV), "Don't you yourselves admit that this Temple, which bears my name, has become a den of thieves? Surely I see all the evil going on there." Somebody once said, if you think everything's fine, you're not paying attention. Jesus ventures one uneasy step further. His actions suggest, if you think everything's fine, you're likely the one who's benefitting.

According to the antipoverty organization Oxfam International, in 2017 "eight billionaires (men) own the same wealth as the 3.6 billion people who make up the poorest half of humanity."[5] Oxfam reports that these super-rich fuel the inequality crisis by dodging taxes and driving down wages. Where are the Christians overturning tables over the growing gap between the rich and the poor? When Christians pretend injustice doesn't exist and don't act to repair it, God's tears flow hard enough to make the oceans rise. "Woe to him who builds his house by unrighteousness, and his upper rooms by injustice; who makes his neighbors work for nothing, and does not give them their wages" (Jeremiah 22:13).

Beware of people who tell you that you can't change the world, for usually those are the very people who don't want to see any part of it changed.

God calls all people of faith to change the world by seeking justice. The Bible couldn't be clearer on this point. To love God is to know God, and to know God is to do justice. "'He gave justice and help to the poor and needy, and everything went well for him. Isn't that what it means to know me?' says the Lord" (Jeremiah 22:16 NLV). As the Christian philosopher Cornel West once said, justice is what love looks like in public.

Justice, in order to be true justice, demands a love for everyone with no exceptions—an equal sharing of mercy as well as all benefits and burdens of life together. In theory, this sounds reasonable and desirable. But in practice, so many people make themselves—or a certain group—the exception. Consider the way the United States has always claimed to be a democracy, meaning everyone has the right to voice and vote, but for centuries, white men didn't allow African Americans or women to possess either. Who are we kidding? Most of us don't want justice. We want *exceptions*.

Injustice is like a koala bear (minus the cuteness). Both are monophagous, meaning they live off only one food. Koalas eat only eucalyptus; injustice survives solely on exceptions.

My colleague the pastor Jim Mauney illustrated this truth in a recent sermon. One day when Jim was a kid, his mom gave him a bag of M&M's and instructed him to share it with his two younger siblings. Jim distributed the M&M's but decided it was only fair for him to keep a few extra for himself, since he was not only the biggest but also the one doing all the work. When Jim's mom found out what he had done, Jim tasted trouble like he'd never seen. His mother forced him to share—equally this time—with his siblings and to hand back the excess M&M's he had greedily hoarded for himself.

Pastor Jim preached, "What I experienced as the pure wrath of Mama, felt like pure love and justice to my brother and sister." A love without exceptions hurts—but only those accustomed to making exceptions.

In theory, justice sounds awesome. *Bring it on!* we say. But in real life, to our surprise, justice—like grace—can hurt big time. As can a love without limits.

For a long, long time in this country, white people made black people the exception to love. Some white people still do—like the KKK, a bunch of white supremacist Christians who hate African Americans and believe God hates them too. Black Lives Matter (BLM) is a movement that tries to assert in the midst of such brokenness that black people should no longer be made the exception to people's (or God's) love. But many white people responded to BLM with rage. But *all* lives matter, they said. BLM never said they didn't. Their point was that black lives mattered *too*.

When Jesus preached his Sermon on the Mount, he declared blessed are the poor, the meek, and the peacemakers. Imagine if counterprotesters had shown up with signs shouting, "NO JESUS, ALL ARE BLESSED." The thought is laughable, yet that is the exact logic of "all lives matter." Jesus never once said blessed are the rich. He didn't have to, because everyone already thought of and treated those folks as supersize-blessed. But the same was not true for the poor and meek. Everyone thought of them as nobodies. This is why Jesus had to shout it from the mountaintop: the poor and meek are blessed (*too*).

To those and only those who have long benefited from a love *with* limits, a love *without* limits feels—paradoxically—like wrath. Or like a new and painful limit. To everyone else, it feels like the blessed day the M&M's finally got handed out fairly.

This is the fallout from a love without limits. Many will sing *alleluia*—but others will cry *oh sh*t*.

Us versus Them

A third way we make God weep today is with our never-ending division of the world into "us" and "them." While I'd like to say I know what to do about this, the truth is, I'm part of the problem.

I once had a student named Darren Rodeo (Rodeo—pronounced ro-day-oh). To borrow a phrase from my Buddhist friend Mia, who is trained in nonviolent communication and is a much better human than I am, Darren was a "person who made my life less than wonderful."[6] Professors aren't supposed to admit they can have students who are thorns in their side, but Darren was definitely mine (sorry, Mia).

One day in religion class, Darren raised his hand and declared, "Of course homosexuality is wrong. Anyone with eyes to see can see that HIV/AIDS is God's curse on homosexuals." Some students in the class were gay. Others weren't, but loved someone who was. Some students and I had just come back from South Africa, where we held HIV-positive babies in our arms and learned that in most countries in the world, children under fourteen and women aged fifteen to twenty-four have the fastest growing rates of HIV/AIDS, primarily because of rape, domestic violence, and being forced into sex-trafficking. For all of us, Darren's words struck a raw nerve of pain.

The weeks to come revealed that on every possible social and political issue known to humanity, Darren Rodeo and I stood on opposite sides of a barbed-wire fence. I knew this, and I'm 99 percent sure Darren knew it as well, for he often gave me Fox News segments to watch. He most likely dug up my views in my books and articles, because I don't teach by bullying, force-feeding the class my perspective, or even by lecturing. Instead, I try to teach by open, democratic dialogue and respectful discussion, so that if/when I do share my views, it's only one view of many (most students are surprised the first time I raise my hand in my own class). As much as I wanted to shut Darren down (or shut him up!), I knew I couldn't. And so, a victim of my own values, every day I was stuck having to hear Darren out—even when it meant sobbing in my office after class.

During those weeks, I knew God wanted me to stretch love's bungee cord far enough to reach Darren Rodeo. And though I tried, it kept breaking. So I devised a new plan. Every day before class, I went down my attendance sheet and prayed for each student by name: "God please be with _____ today. Help me to love [her/him]." I didn't pray to like them—in at least one case, that felt impossible—but to *love* them. Each time I got to Darren's name, I grimaced but said the words anyway.

One day during my prayers, a revelation struck me: the reason God made love a *commandment* and not a fun intramural option like flag football was because of the Darren Rodeos in our lives. If love for people-who-make-our-lives-less-than-wonderful was a choice, well, God knew, no one would ever sign up. Love's not extracurricular; it's *the* curriculum.

Finally the agonizing semester came to an end, and grades were due. I never grade students on whether they agree with me or not—again, tempting!—but on their work's quality, and undeniably, Darren was a good student. And so, though it hurt a bit to do so, I submitted the A- Darren had earned. Then I did a Snoopy happy dance in my office at the thought of never seeing him again. (Did I just admit that?)

A year later, the registrar sent me my new Christian Ethics class roster. As my eyes scrolled down, I spotted the name of doom: Darren Rodeo. *Unbelievable,* I thought, *why on earth would he ever want to take a class with me again?*

About halfway through the new semester, we had a class discussion about capital punishment. I suspected Darren would be a strong proponent, but instead, something unexpected happened. Darren Rodeo sat silent, staring down at his pen. I wanted to write his pale face off as a hangover from the previous night's frat party, but in spite of myself, I worried. After class I asked, "Hey Darren, you okay?"

"Yeah," he mumbled, and walked out. I hung around the classroom a little longer to gather my things, and then left. To my surprise, Darren was waiting in the hall for me. And—what?—he was crying.

"Dr. Bussie," he said. "I have to tell you something. I had a huge fight with my stepsister two days ago and this morning I got a call. She . . . she . . . she tried to kill herself last night." His shoulders heaved. "I wanted to tell you . . . because I don't know who to go to . . . and I knew you . . . well, I knew you would care."

And just like that, I could admit for the first time ever that not only was Darren Rodeo right, he also knew something I didn't. I *did* care (but only because he cared first). Enough to stand in that hall, high heels and all, talking for ninety more minutes. And so many more times after that.

I don't know if prayers change the world, but I do know they change the person who says them. I know, because that day in the hallway, my heart nearly broke out of love for Darren Rodeo.

Loving those we like feels so easy. Like slipping into our favorite pair of comfy jeans. Loving those we don't? Like trying to fit a pair of babyGap jeans onto a hippo.

The famous Christian ethicist Reinhold Niebuhr once declared that love is the impossible possibility. When he said it, he must have been thinking about how mind-bendingly difficult it is to love people who don't live, think, act, or believe like we do.

These are the folks most of us mark with *agape*'s asterisk, either by our thoughts or actions. We reason: when Jesus commanded *Love the whole world, no exceptions*, he couldn't have meant *them*, right?

A lot of Christians have no problem loving Jesus; it's other people we can't stand.

Back to Niebuhr. Niebuhr, who believed war was sometimes justified, often got in huge arguments with pacifists, who believed war was always wrong. Though Niebuhr completely disagreed with pacifists, he regularly expressed how much he appreciated and valued them. He argued that his opponents should never be silenced, because, "we need their testimony against us . . . lest we ever become callous to the horror of war, and lest we forget the ambiguity of our own actions and motives."[7]

More than ever, we need to take a cue from Niebuhr. Next time you're demonizing someone, force yourself to find—and even state aloud—something valuable about their position or them as a person. Challenge yourself to remember their shared humanity. Of all the things we do today that make God grieve, our refusal to even attempt to do this anymore must top the list.

Our puny, pint-sized love these days is like those dreadful drug commercials where the high-speed voiceover lists an absurdly long litany of side effects from diarrhea to death. God's love, however, is disclaimer and asterisk-free. Added bonus: mere *existence* is the only insurance we'll ever need for a lifetime supply.

While we never seem to be able to jump the final hurdle, Jesus' Olympic love runs hard toward the high bar that separates "us" from "them," and vaults right over it. Successfully. Gracefully. Every time. The apostle Paul writes, "For he [Jesus] is our peace; in his flesh he has made both groups into one and has broken down the dividing wall, that is, the hostility between us. He has abolished the law . . . so that he might create in himself one new humanity in place of the two, thus making peace, and might reconcile both groups to God in one body through the cross, thus putting to death that hostility through it" (Ephesians 2:14–16).

On the cross, then, something else died in addition to Jesus: the ugly wall of us-versus-them that divided the Jews and gentiles back in the day. In our day too, so many us-versus-thems divide, begging for reconciliation. So many walls—each so painstakingly built. Operating in our culture today is a lie so powerful it plays like a law: if we disagree or are different, we must hate each other. This is a law Christians must break every day, as Jesus himself did.

According to Ephesians, Jesus is the ultimate iconoclast who smashes every hostile us-versus-them wall we've ever built, and plants peace in its place. He exposes the dichotomies we cling to for what they always were: lies, superiority trips, and pious justifications for harm and violence against our "thems." Through Jesus, our atonement—literally our at-one-ment—with God is achieved.

But that's not all, says Paul. Jesus' life and death also achieve our atonement—our at oneness—*with each other*. "There is no longer Jew or Greek, there is no longer slave or free, there is no longer male and female; for all of you are one in Christ Jesus" (Galatians 3:28).

Jesus brings peace and reconciliation because he unveils our true wholeness, our unity with God and one another. In both the original languages of the Bible, the words for peace mean so much more than simply *not at war*. The Hebrew *shalom* means *wholeness* and *relationship*, and the Greek word for peace, *eirene*, comes from the verb *to join, to make one*.

Think of the worst division in your life. Now think this: the unity for which your heart so longs has, in a very real way, already happened. The question is not, *When* will we all be reconciled? It's, *How* will we live into the truth that we are already one? "As it is, there are many members, yet one body. The eye cannot say to the hand, 'I have no need of you,' nor again the head to the feet, 'I have no need of you'" (1 Corinthians 12:20–21). We're all interconnected, and we can't live without one another, but only a love without limits accepts this. A love without limits proclaims, *there is no me without you, and I vow to live like it.*

Every time and every place you smash down the wall of the us-versus-them lie to build peace, you live into Jesus' love without limits. Don't expect most people to get this, though, or to thank you. In the 1950s, many white folks labeled the Reverend Martin Luther King Jr. an extremist and enemy of the state. Our own government treated King like a terrorist, monitoring his every action, once even sending him a letter calling him an evil, abnormal beast and moral imbecile.[8]

Real peace-building disturbs the peace because it always begins with the unmasking of injustice. (Typically: other people are not less than us and they do not deserve the crap we're dishing them.) Most people misunderstand peace as nothing more than the absence of conflict or disagreement. But that kind of so-called peace is nothing more than a status quo popsicle.

So much of what passes for peace in this world is frozen injustice—popped in the freezer by privileged folks like me whom it benefits, and sold in a bright-colored wrapper of acceptability. In the words of the prophet Jeremiah (6:14), "They have treated the wound of my people carelessly, saying peace, peace where there is no peace." Followers of a love-without-limits God don't seek peace. Instead, they seek a just peace—meaning, a peace built upon the foundations of justice.

A magnificent description of what living a love without limits looks like appears in Acts. In chapter 17, Paul and Silas travel to Thessalonica and begin to share Jesus' message of radical love at their friend Jason's house. The authorities hear about it and, as per uzhe, lose their marbles. They hunt Paul and Silas and shout, "These people who have been turning the world upside down have come here also, and Jason has entertained them as guests" (Acts 17:6–7). What a beautiful description of who Christians should be: people who turn the world upside down. Especially by loving those we're taught not to love, as Jesus himself did: "The Spirit of the Lord . . . has anointed me to bring good news to the poor. He has sent me to proclaim release to the captives and recovery of sight to the blind, to let the oppressed go free" (Luke 4:18).

All of these things that grieve God are so important to remember, but we can't let them become a single story. We must also remember the thousands of things people do that make God do a divine happy dance. All across the world, every single day, amazing people turn the world upside down. They're ripping off labels. They're practicing resurrection.[9] They're the rock-star teachers of a love without limits.

Take, for example, the African American police officer Leroy Smith. On July 18, 2015, a scorching hot day in Columbia, South Carolina, Officer Smith was standing in front of the statehouse watching a Ku Klux Klan rally. Hate and white supremacy were everywhere: on lips, T-shirts, banners, and signs. When Smith saw a white Klan member begin to pass out from heat stroke, he helped him get to water and shelter. This image of a love without limits, captured on Twitter, went viral.[10]

Or take Nadine Collier. Her mother, Ethel Lance, was killed on June 17, 2015, at Emanuel AME Church in Charleston, South Carolina, when a white teenager walked into her Bible study and, after expressing hatred of African Americans, murdered her and eight other people. At the hearing, Nadine looked straight at her mother's killer and shocked the nation by saying, "You took something very precious from me. I will never talk to her again. I will never, ever hold her again. But I forgive you. And have mercy on your soul."[11]

And don't forget Rose Mapendo, a human rights activist from the Democratic Republic of Congo, who recently spoke at my college. In 1994, the Hutu declared a genocide of the Tutsi in the region. Rose, a Tutsi, and her husband and seven kids were immediately sent to a concentration camp. At the prison, a camp commander murdered Rose's husband while she watched. Another camp commander demanded that she exchange her daughter's virginity for her son's life. One night Rose, who was pregnant, gave birth to twins on the cold, dirty floor of her shared prison cell. In an act of radical forgiveness, Rose, a Christian, named each twin after one of the camps' cruel commanders.

Incredibly, this worked. The wife of one of the commanders brought food and clothing to Rose. That commander, who was eventually ordered to kill all remaining prisoners, instead transferred Rose's family to another prison, saying that he couldn't bear to kill his own namesake. Within several weeks of arriving at the new camp, Rose and her kids were transferred again, but this time to a Red Cross human rights center. As a part of the United States' emergency resettlement program of Tutsi refugees, Rose and all nine of her children eventually made it to the States. In 2009, Rose won the UN Humanitarian of the Year award for the refugee aid foundation she established.

Rose, like Leroy and Nadine, solved faith's secret and she asks us to live it: *Forgiveness is love's sweetest revenge.*

$$\backsim$$

I want to leave you with one last hope story—one about this book itself, and how the love I received helped me to forgive its censors.

When I refused to cave in to my original publisher's censorship demands, I lost a lot more than my contract, cash, book rights, and dignity. I lost the most important thing of all: hope. Given all the other countless headlines of hate, I began to fear that love with exceptions had won, and love without limits had lost. Shame, silence, and sadness sank me in their undertow. For months, I couldn't even bear to tell anyone my story. That is, until one day, a friend encouraged me to write about it.

Desperate for air, I took her advice. I sat down and scribbled out my story in a short blog. Next, in black Sharpie I wrote CENSORED on a piece of duct tape, stuck it across my mouth, and took a selfie. Then, I posted both the blog and photo on Facebook. (You've seen that selfie and read that post. It's this book's introduction.)

What happened next took my breath away. Within only a few hours, the post went viral. People liked, loved, shared, re-shared, and commented. They told me they loved me and that I was not alone. They made me laugh with posts bearing the new hashtag #LoveLikeTheFreakinSun. They made me cry with posts like this one from a LGBTQ friend: *Thank you for not deleting us.* Some people (Samaritans!) tagged people they hoped could help. A woman I'd never even met tagged some folks at Fortress Press. And that's how it happened that Tony, Fortress's senior acquisitions editor, saw my post.

On the very same day as my post, Tony happened to be nine hundred miles away from his office and—*wait for it*—sitting right next to my agent at a writer's conference. Tony turned to my agent and asked, "Hey, do you know who Jacqueline Bussie's agent is?" After my agent identified himself, he emailed Tony and the Fortress team *Love Without Limits.* Fortress made an offer to buy the book the very next day. Yes, you heard me right: *in only twenty-four hours,* my Facebook squad found this book a new publisher. This story of hope is so real, you're holding its ending in your hands.

Once all the paperwork was signed and we'd bought my book's rights back, I gave my Facebook community a thousand thank-yous. I knew I could never repay their love without limits. So I decided to do the next best thing: live in a way that was worthy of it. For starters, I forgave my original publisher. Then, I promised to remember the lessons this experience taught me. And now, I entrust them to you.

1. Your story matters. Tell it.
2. Cornel West was right. Now more than ever, what the world needs most is more people who are *not for sale.*
3. Never cave to the lie you can't make a difference. Even a click or share can jump-start a heart.
4. At times, you may feel powerless, but you're not. The power to tell the tale of why you feel powerless never leaves you.
5. Hope is a map. If you ever lose yours, you can always share mine. What matters is we all find our way home.

And last but not least:

6. Hope wins. Always.

NOTES

Chapter 1

1. In order to protect people's privacy, certain names and identifying details in this book have been changed.

Chapter 2

1. Julia Cameron, *The Right to Write: An Invitation and Initiation into the Writing Life* (New York: Tarcher/Putnam, 1998), 31.
2. Cameron, *Right to Write*, 101.

Chapter 3

1. Martin Luther King Jr., "A Christmas Sermon," December 24, 1967, The King Center, https://tinyurl.com/yanptjm7.

Chapter 4

1. Karen McVeigh, "Church of England to Consider Transgender Naming Ceremony," *The Guardian*, May 21, 2015, https://tinyurl.com/y9lu46o9.
2. Susan Musgrove, "After My Sex Change I'm Now a Woman in the Eyes of God," *The Telegraph*, April 20, 2013, https://tinyurl.com/ybo3cljd.
3. Frederick Buechner, *Secrets in the Dark: A Life in Sermons* (New York: HarperSanFrancisco, 2006), 170.
4. Rabbi Benjamin Blech, "Judaism and the Power of Names," Aish.com, April 20, 2013, https://tinyurl.com/ycw2vvrx.

5. Julia K. Dinsmore, *My Name is Child of God . . . Not "Those People": A First-Person Look at Poverty* (Minneapolis: Augsburg, 2007).
6. Don Mackenzie, Ted Falcon, and Jamal Rahman, *Getting to the Heart of Interfaith: The Eye-Opening, Hope-Filled Friendship of a Pastor, a Rabbi, and a Sheikh* (Woodstock, VT: SkyLight Paths, 2009), 72.
7. Mackenzie, Falcon, and Rahman, *Getting to the Heart*, 148.

Chapter 5

1. Karl Barth, *The Doctrine of God*, vol. 2, part 2 of *Church Dogmatics*, edited by G. W. Bromiley and T. F. Torrance (Edinburgh: T&T Clark, 1957), 13.
2. Mary O'Hara, "The LGBT Couples Adopting 'Hard to Place' Children," *The Guardian*, March 4, 2015, https://tinyurl.com/y9jjvakr.
3. Bob Grant, "Zeroing in on the Gay Gene," *The Scientist*, November 19, 2014, https://tinyurl.com/yce2lm6q.
4. See for example the article, "1500 Animal Species Practice Homosexuality," Medical Science News, October 23, 2006, https://tinyurl.com/y7t6vzzq.

Chapter 6

1. Chimamanda Ngozi Adichie, "The Danger of a Single Story," TEDx Talks, YouTube video, 19:16, uploaded by TED, October 7, 2009, https://tinyurl.com/kvj8lp4.
2. Amber Phillips, "Americans Are Increasingly Skeptical of Muslims. But Most Americans Don't Talk to Muslims," *Washington Post*, July 15, 2016, https://tinyurl.com/yc2xlrw9.
3. Amani Al-Khatahtbeh, *Muslim Girl: A Coming of Age* (New York: Simon & Schuster, 2016), 17.
4. John Renard, *Understanding the Islamic Experience* (New York: Paulist, 2002), 139. Also found in Sahih Muslim, *The Book of Repentance* (4:1642, no. 22).
5. This cartoon is reprinted with full permission from cartoonist Malcolm Evans. Permission granted via personal email correspondence, September 16, 2017. It should be noted that the

garment worn by the Muslim woman in this image is technically a niqab, not a burka. A burka covers the entire face, including the eyes.

6. See www.headcoveringmovement.com.

7. See Rob Bell, *Love Wins: A Book about Heaven, Hell, and the Fate of Every Person Who Ever Lived* (New York: HarperOne, 2011), 7.

8. The five countries are Turkey, Bangladesh, Pakistan, Indonesia, and Kosovo.

9. Aroosa Shaukat, "Human Chain Formed to Protect Christians during Lahore Mass," *The Express Tribune*, October 6, 2013, https://tinyurl.com/yd9jwgxe.

10. Vic Micolucci, "Medical Mecca: Muslims Quietly Serving Jacksonville Community," News4Jax, January 20, 2017, https://tinyurl.com/y85jnyc3.

11. Brian D. McLaren, *Why Did Jesus, Moses, the Buddha, and Mohammed Cross the Road? Christian Identity in a Multi-Faith World* (New York: Jericho, 2012), 228.

12. R.T. Anderson, *The International Standard Bible Encyclopedia*, s.v. "Samaritan," (Grand Rapids, MI: Eerdmans, 1988), 307.

13. "Holy Envy Explained by Krister Stendahl," YouTube video, 3:17, uploaded by Brian Payne, June 17, 2016, https://tinyurl.com/ybwwdfvy.

Chapter 7

1. James A. Metzger, *Consumption and Wealth in Luke's Travel Narrative* (Leiden: Brill, 2007), 28.

2. G. K. Chesterton, *The Paradoxes of Mr. Pond* (Los Angeles: Indo-European Publishing, 2011), 42.

3. Fun fact: North of Normal is the city of Fargo's tagline.

Chapter 8

1. C. S. Lewis, *Mere Christianity* (New York: HarperCollins, 1980), 125, 127.

2. Lewis, *Mere Christianity*, 121–22.

3. C. S. Lewis, *The Four Loves* (New York: Harcourt Brace, 1960), 134.
4. Valerie Saiving Goldstein, "The Human Situation: A Feminine View," *The Journal of Religion* 40, no. 2 (April 1960): 100–112.
5. Dietrich Bonhoeffer, *Letters and Papers from Prison* (New York: Touchstone, 1997), 17.
6. "Glamour Relationship Abuse Survey: Nearly 60 Percent of Young Women Have Experienced Abuse," *Huffington Post*, May 4, 2011, https://tinyurl.com/y9egtla4.
7. Madeline L'Engle, *Walking on Water: Reflections on Faith and Art* (Wheaton, IL: Harold Shaw, 1980), 69.

Chapter 9

1. Martín Prechtel, *The Smell of Rain on Dust: Grief and Praise* (Berkeley, CA: North Atlantic, 2015), 36.
2. Prechtel, *Smell of Rain*, 35.
3. Ellen Painter Dollar, "Can Hospitality Be Too Scruffy?," *Patheos* (blog), June 19, 2014, https://tinyurl.com/ybelhymh.
4. If you're thinking about trying it, you can find a wonderful sample worship service online here: Rev. Nancy C. Townely, "Blue Christmas," Cokesbury, PDF, https://tinyurl.com/y83y4vqu.
5. This quote has been used in several iterations by many activist groups (including the Zapatista movement fighting for indigenous people in Mexico in the '90s). The original quote comes from Greek poet Dinos Christianopoulos, who was marginalized in Greece in the 1970s for being gay, in his collection Μικρα ποιηματα. The poem can be read in its original Greek on the University of Athens archives: https://tinyurl.com/y79sz9o8.

Chapter 10

1. This popular story can be found in multiple sources. For example, Marc H. Tanenbaum, *A Prophet for Our Time: An Anthology of the Writings of Rabbi Marc H. Tanenbaum*, ed. Judith H. Banki and Eugene J. Fisher (New York: Fordham University Press, 2002), 183.

2. Shane Claiborne, "The Scandal of Grace" (public lecture, Concordia College, Moorhead, Minnesota, April 15, 2014).

3. John Burnett, "Statue of a Homeless Jesus Startles a Wealthy Community," NPR, April 13, 2014, https://tinyurl.com/y9styhc7.

4. Tim Chester, "'Homeless Jesus' Sculpture Banned from Central London," Mashable, April 26, 2016, https://tinyurl.com/ybdb9vuu.

5. "Just 8 Men Own Same Wealth as Half the World," Oxfam International, January 16, 2017, https://tinyurl.com/ydalkwmh.

6. This phrase comes from Marshall Rosenberg, the founder of Nonviolent Communication. See Marshall B. Rosenberg, "Being Me, Loving You: A Simple Exercise to Inspire Connection with a Loved One," Puddle Dancer Press, https://tinyurl.com/yagx8drd.

7. Reinhold Niebuhr, "Why the Christian Church Is Not Pacifist," in *The Essential Reinhold Niebuhr: Selected Essays and Addresses*, ed. Robert McAfee Brown (New Haven: Yale University Press, 1986), 119.

8. Beverly Gage, "What an Uncensored Letter to M.L.K. Reveals," *New York Times Magazine*, November 11, 2014, https://tinyurl.com/ybjfb5vb.

9. The phrase "practice resurrection" comes from poet Wendell Berry.

10. Dominique Mosbergen, "Viral Photo Shows Black Police Officer Helping White Supremacist," *Huffington Post*, July 20, 2015, https://tinyurl.com/y84wqkdx.

11. Mark Berman, "'I Forgive You.' Relatives of Charleston Church Shooting Victims Address Dylann Roof," *Washington Post*, June 19, 2015, https://tinyurl.com/y9uaf6q7.